ZAGATSURVEY.

VANCOUVER RESTAURANTS
Plus Nightlife, Attractions
and Hotels

**Local Editors: Tim Pawsey, Heather Pawsey
and Carolyn B. Heller**

Editor: Betsy Andrews

Published and distributed by
ZAGAT SURVEY, LLC
4 Columbus Circle
New York, New York 10019
Tel: 212 977 6000
E-mail: vancouver@zagat.com
Web site: www.zagat.com

Acknowledgments

We thank Michaela Albert, Talia Albert, Sue Alexander, Linda Barnard, Dorothy Budden, Steven Shukow and Nancy Won. We are also grateful to our assistant editors, Victoria Elmacioglu and Josh Rogers, as well as the following members of our staff: Maryanne Bertollo, Reni Chin, Liz Daleske, Schuyler Frazier, Jeff Freier, Natalie Lebert, Mike Liao, Dave Makulec, Robert Poole, Thomas Sheehan, Joshua Siegel, Kelly Stewart, Sharon Yates and Kyle Zolner.

Contents

About This Survey

Here are the results of our *Vancouver Restaurant Survey*, covering 248 restaurants, bars and attractions as tested by 1,759 locals. We've also included a selection of top hotels as rated by avid travelers.

This marks the 27th year that Zagat Survey has reported on the shared experiences of people like you. What started in 1979 as a hobby rating NYC restaurants has come a long way. Today we have over 250,000 active surveyors and now cover dining, entertaining, golf, hotels, resorts, spas, movies, music, nightlife, shopping, theater and tourist attractions. All of these guides are based on consumer surveys. They are also available by subscription at zagat.com, and for use on PDAs and cell phones.

By regularly surveying large numbers of customers, we hope to have achieved a uniquely current and reliable series of guides. Our editors have synopsized our surveyors' opinions, with their comments shown in quotation marks. We sincerely thank each of these people; this book is really "theirs."

We are especially grateful to our editors, Tim Pawsey, a columnist at the *Vancouver Courier*; Heather Pawsey, a classical singer with a journalistic and public relations background and a passionate interest in food and wine; and Carolyn B. Heller, Zagat's former Boston editor, who contributes food and travel articles to such publications as Vancouver-based *Harmony In-Flight Magazine.*

**Finally, we invite you to join any of our upcoming *Surveys* –
to do so, just register at zagat.com.** Each participant will receive a free copy of the resulting guide when it is published. Your comments and even criticisms of this guide are also solicited. There is always room for improvement with your help. Just contact us at vancouver@zagat.com.

New York, NY
June 26, 2006

Nina and Tim Zagat

What's New

Almost 40% of Vancouver surveyors report eating out more than they did two years ago, and it's easy to see why: with stellar seasonal Pacific Northwest fare and a burgeoning wine industry, Vancouver, Victoria and Whistler have emerged as culinary destinations, and their appeal keeps growing.

Water, Water Everywhere: Diners can take advantage of copious ocean and harbour views from waterside rooms. New shore dwellers include Downtown Eclectic Nu, and for Pacific Northwest dishes, Ocean 6 Seventeen at Stamp's Landing and Watermark on Kits Beach.

Small Plates, Big Trend: The tapas mania, started at Bin 941, has spread throughout Vancouver. Asian small plates are on order at East Sider Ch'i, hipsters share Eclectic bites at the East Side's Habit Lounge and foodies fawn over unique flavours at Downtown Pacific Northwest spot Rare. The Japanese-nibbles *izakaya* craze has been imported to Downtown's Kitanoya Guu and its two siblings, along with Yaletown's Shiru-Bay Chopstick Café.

Growth Spurt: There's a restaurant and nightlife boom in the city. Downtown dining arrivals include Saltlik Steakhouse, and Nuevo Latino Century helps drive a Crosstown revival. West Coast–centric Aurora Bistro is pulling in East Siders, while West Siders welcome the Iberian Senova. To Vancouver's clubland come the trendy Yaletowner Opus Bar and Downtown's live-music venue Cellar Nightclub.

Sea or Ski: BC weekenders dine and wine in style. On Vancouver Island, locally sourced fare lures patrons to Brentwood Bay Lodge's Arbutus Grille and Esquimalt's Rosemeade. Modern Europeanist Après lives up to its name as Whistler's post-ski magnet, while the Four Seasons' Fifty Two 80 tops all ratings for elegant mountain meals.

Vancouver   Tim Pawsey
June 26, 2006   Heather Pawsey

Vancouver's Most Popular

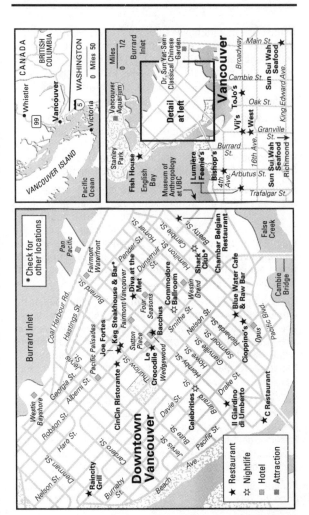

Map details (top left inset):

CANADA
BRITISH COLUMBIA
WASHINGTON
Whistler
Vancouver
Victoria
VANCOUVER ISLAND
Pacific Ocean
Miles 0 — 50
99
5

Vancouver (top right inset):

Burrard Inlet
Miles 0 — 1/2
Dr. Sun Yat-Sen Classical Chinese Garden
Detail at left
Vancouver Aquarium
Stanley Park
Fish House
English Bay
Museum of Anthropology at UBC
Lumière
Feenie's
Bishop's
Burrard St.
4th Ave.
Arbutus St.
Trafalgar St.
Main St.
Broadway
Sun Sui Wah Seafood
Cambie St.
Tojo's
Oak St.
King Edward Ave.
Vij's
West
Granville St.
16th Ave.
Sun Sui Wah Seafood
Richmond

Downtown Vancouver (bottom map):

* Check for other locations

Burrard Inlet
Pan Pacific
Fairmont Waterfront
Burrard St.
Hastings St.
Coal Harbour Rd.
Jervis St.
Pacific Palisades
Keg Steakhouse & Bar*
Joe Fortes
Sutton Place
Le Crocodile
Wedgewood
CinCin Ristorante
Bute St.
Thurlow St.
Georgia St.
Alberni St.
Robson St.
Haro St.
Nelson St.
Denman St.
Cardero St.
Burnaby St.
Raincity Grill
Beach Ave.
Davie St.
Downtown Vancouver
Pacific St.
Celebrities
Hornby St.
Howe St.
Burrard St.
Drake St.
Il Giardino di Umberto
C Restaurant
Pender St.
Homer St.
Cambie St.
Beatty St.
Dunsmuir St.
Hamilton St.
Diva at the Met
Fairmont Vancouver
Four Seasons
Bacchus
Commodore Ballroom
Westin Grand
Smithe St.
Nelson St.
Seymour St.
Granville St.
Richards St.
Shark Club
Chambar Belgian Restaurant
False Creek
Cambie Bridge
Blue Water Cafe & Raw Bar
Cioppino's
Opus
Pacific Blvd.
Westin Bayshore

★ Restaurant
☆ Nightlife
■ Hotel
■ Attraction

Vancouver's Most Popular

Each surveyor has been asked to name his or her five favourite restaurants. This list reflects their choices.

1. Lumière
2. C Restaurant
3. West
4. Bishop's
5. Vij's
6. Le Crocodile
7. ToJo's
8. CinCin
9. Keg Steakhouse
10. Joe Fortes
11. Feenie's
12. Raincity Grill
13. Chambar
14. Blue Water Cafe
15. Cioppino's
16. Sun Sui Wah
17. Il Giardino/Umberto
18. Bacchus
19. Fish House
20. Diva at the Met

It's obvious that many of the restaurants on the above list are among Vancouver's most expensive, but if popularity were calibrated to price, we suspect that a number of other restaurants would join the above ranks. Given the fact that both our surveyors and readers love to discover dining bargains, we have added a list of Top Bangs for the Buck on page 9. These are restaurants that give real quality at extremely reasonable prices.

The map on the facing page includes Vancouver's Most Popular restaurants, nightspots and attractions, as well as some top hotels. See page 53 for a list of Vancouver's Most Popular nightlife venues, and page 59 for a list of Vancouver's Most Popular attractions.

Top Restaurant Ratings

Excluding places with low voting. Top ratings for Victoria & Vancouver Island and Whistler can be found on page 10.

Top Food

29 West	C Restaurant
28 Lumière	**25** Caffe de Medici
Bishop's	Raincity Grill
Vij's	Parkside
Pear Tree	Bin 941/942
27 ToJo's	Five Sails
Le Crocodile	Kitanoya Guu
La Regalade	Aurora Bistro
26 Cioppino's	Chartwell*
Il Giardino/Umberto	Kirin Mandarin*
Villa del Lupo	Morton's Steak*
Vij's Rangoli	Blue Water Cafe
Diva at the Met	Go Fish!
Cru	Bistro Pastis
Gotham Steak	Chambar

By Cuisine

Chinese
- **25** Kirin Mandarin
- **24** Imperial Chinese
- Sun Sui Wah
- **23** Shanghai Chinese
- Kirin Seafood

Eclectic
- **25** Bin 941/942
- **23** Trafalgar's Bistro
- Stella's
- **22** Nu
- glowbal grill

French
- **28** Lumière
- **27** Le Crocodile
- La Regalade
- **25** Five Sails
- Bistro Pastis

Italian
- **26** Il Giardino/Umberto
- Villa del Lupo
- **25** Caffe de Medici
- **24** Lombardo's
- Circolo

---

* Indicates a tie with restaurant above

subscribe to zagat.com

Japanese

27 ToJo's
25 Kitanoya Guu
    Shiru-Bay Chopstick
24 Gyoza King
    EN Japanese

Pacific Northwest

29 West
26 Diva at the Met
25 Raincity Grill
    Aurora Bistro
    Chartwell*

Seafood

26 C Restaurant
25 Blue Water Cafe
    Go Fish!
24 Pajo's
    Cannery

Steakhouses

26 Gotham Steak
25 Morton's Steak
23 Hy's
    Kobe Japanese
21 Joe Fortes

Top Decor

27 Watermark/Kits
    Lift
26 Bacchus
    West
    Sequoia Grill
    Five Sails
25 Coast

    Seasons Hill Top
    Gotham Steak
    Circolo
    Chartwell
24 Il Giardino/Umberto
    C Restaurant
    Salmon House

Top Service

27 Bishop's
    West
    Caffe de Medici
    Pear Tree*
    Chartwell
26 Lumière
    Five Sails

    Villa del Lupo
    Le Crocodile
    C Restaurant
    Bacchus
25 Parkside
    Morton's Steak
    Fleuri

Top Bangs for the Buck

1. Nat's NY Pizzeria
2. Pajo's
3. Vera's Burger
4. Go Fish!
5. Shao-Lin Noodle
6. Vij's Rangoli
7. Tomahawk BBQ
8. Kitanoya Guu
9. Habibi's
10. Lombardo's

Victoria & Vancouver Island

Most Popular
1. Keg Steakhouse
2. Sooke Harbour
3. Empress Room
4. Il Terrazzo
5. Cafe Brio

Top Food
27 Hastings House
    Camille's
    Zambri's
    Rosemeade
    Paprika Bistro

Top Decor
28 Pointe/Wickaninnish
    Empress Room
27 Rosemeade
26 Hastings House
25 Aerie Resort

Top Service
28 Hastings House
26 Aerie Resort
    Sooke Harbour
    Empress Room
    Rosemeade

Whistler

Most Popular
1. Keg Steakhouse
2. Rim Rock Cafe
3. Araxi
4. La Rua
5. Trattoria/Umberto

Top Food
27 Fifty Two 80 Bistro
26 Rim Rock Cafe
    Trattoria/Umberto
25 Il Caminetto/Umberto
    Araxi

Top Decor
27 Fifty Two 80 Bistro
23 Araxi
    La Rua
    Rim Rock Cafe
    Après

Top Service
27 Fifty Two 80 Bistro
24 Rim Rock Cafe
    La Rua
23 Trattoria/Umberto
    Hy's

Ratings & Symbols

Name, Address, Phone Number & Web Site

Hours & Credit Cards

Zagat Ratings

F	D	S	$
▽ 23	9	13	$15

Tim & Nina's ◑ ⊠ ⇭

8 Paradise Pl. (Seaweed St.), 250-555-1234; www.zagat.com

The "cute" trained harbour seal "really knows how to muddle a mojito" at this "quirky" Asian–Pacific Northwest tapas lounge, serving "totally responsible" organic squid-ink noodles and the like in a Downtown room "the size of a Whistler gondola"; though some suggest T & N "might do better in Surrey", others allow "faded fusion" is "better than foraging in Stanley Park."

Review, with surveyors' comments in quotes

Top Spots: Places with the highest overall ratings, popularity and importance are printed in BLOCK CAPITAL LETTERS.

Hours: ◑ serves after 11 PM, ⊠ closed on Sunday

Credit Cards: ⇭ no credit cards accepted

Ratings are on a scale of **0** to **30. Cost ($)** reflects our surveyors' average estimate (in Canadian dollars) of the price of a dinner with one drink and tip and is a benchmark only. Lunch is usually 25% less.

F	Food	D	Decor	S	Service	$	Cost
23		9		13		$15	

0–9	poor to fair	**20–25**	very good to excellent
10–15	fair to good	**26–30**	extraordinary to perfection
16–19	good to very good	▽	low response/less reliable

For newcomers or survey write-ins listed without ratings, the price range is indicated as follows:

I	$20 and below	**E**	$41 to $60
M	$21 to $40	**VE**	$61 or more

Restaurants

VANCOUVER

Adesso Bistro ▽ 24 | 16 | 19 | $44
2201 W. 1st Ave. (Yew St.), 604-738-6515; www.adessobistro.com
"Finally, a fresh option for sophisticated Italian", this "upscale"
West Side bistro where the signature *stuffata* (braised short ribs
over pappardelle) and "decent" wines earn praise; the room is
"small" but "comfy" ("great patio", too), so *amici* say this "new
kid on the block" shows "promise."

Amarcord 21 | 18 | 23 | $42
104-1168 Hamilton St. (bet. Davie & Helmcken Sts.), 604-681-6500;
www.amarcord.ca
Chef-owner Manlio Mocchi's "gracious welcome" to his "intimate",
"unpretentious" trattoria is the "perfect antidote" to "too-hip
Yaletown"; regulars remember "consistently delicious", "traditional" Italian food and a "top-notch" staff, forgiving decor that's
"a bit dated."

Aqua Riva 20 | 23 | 20 | $43
200 Granville St. (W. Cordova St.), 604-683-5599; www.aquariva.com
"Get a window seat" for rotisseried meats, "wonderful pizzas"
and "fresh fish with a view" at this Downtown Pacific Northwest
"mainstay on the waterfront"; set in an "upbeat", "high-tech"
room with "servers who know their menus", it's "an easy choice for
business" or "out-of-town guests", even if some sniff "tourist trap."

Aurora Bistro 25 | 19 | 21 | $46
2420 Main St. (bet. E. Broadway & E. 8th Ave.), 604-873-9944;
www.aurorabistro.ca
Jeff Van Geest creates "art on your plate" with "first-rate" Pacific
Northwest fare that's "adventurous" and served in "minimalist"
East Side surroundings; the "ethical" kitchen emphasizes "sustainable", "local ingredients", matched with "fine BC wines", and

the "knowledgeable" staff makes everyone "feel welcome" in the newly "cool neighbourhood."

BACCHUS
24 | 26 | 26 | $59

Wedgewood Hotel, 845 Hornby St. (bet. Robson & Smithe Sts.), 604-608-5319; www.wedgewoodhotel.com

"Oozing "old world charm in a New Age city", this "luxurious" Downtowner "breathes power" for "Hollywood stars" and their "bankers, lawyers and brokers"; whether for a "swank" meal in the "gorgeous" dining room or a nightcap by the fire in the "relaxed" piano bar, the passionate propose its "sensual surroundings", "stellar service" and "sublime" French fare "for celebrating a special anniversary" – or to "make up for an infidelity."

Bacchus Bistro
– | – | – | E

Domaine de Chaberton, 1064 216th St. (16th Ave.), Langley, 604-530-9694; www.domainedechaberton.com

This "undiscovered diamond" among the vines at Domaine de Chaberton Winery "in the heart of horse country" pairs "amazing flavours" with "top-notch" service; the few surveyors who've savoured lunch on the patio toast chef Frederic Desbiens' "artfully presented" French bistro plates matched with the property's wines; N.B. dinner Friday and Saturday only.

Beach House at Dundarave Pier
21 | 24 | 22 | $51

150 25th St. (Bellevue Ave.), West Vancouver, 604-922-1414; www.atthebeachhouse.com

"Watch the sun set" from this "beautiful" Pacific Northwester on the West Vancouver waterfront where the seafood is "worth every bite", the wine list is "fabulous" and the service always "friendly"; even sightseers who say the food isn't as "memorable" as the "gorgeous" Burrard Inlet vistas agree that the prix fixe is a "great value."

Beach Side Cafe
21 | 20 | 20 | $45

1362 Marine Dr. (bet. 13th & 14th Sts.), West Vancouver, 604-925-1945; www.beachsidecafe.ca

After several chef changes, this West Vancouver "classic" near Ambleside Beach is "back in top form", drawing Downtowners "across the bridge" for Pacific Northwest fare; it's "especially good for lunch" when you can enjoy the "stunning" "water view" from the rear patio.

Bin 941 Tapas Parlour ☽   25 | 19 | 19 | $36 |
941 Davie St. (bet. Burrard & Howe Sts.), 604-683-1246
Bin 942 Tapas Parlour ☽
1521 W. Broadway (bet. Fir & Granville Sts.), 604-734-9421
www.bin941.com
"Be ready to cuddle up to strangers" – you'll almost "be sitting on
their laps" – at Gord Martin's "boisterous" West End and West
Side "shoeboxes"; "ingenious" Eclectic small plates like Digby
scallops wrapped in prawns put these "funky" joints "at the top
of the tapas bin", though some yearn for "a side of earplugs" and
lament "if only there were a secret password to get a table."

BISHOP'S   28 | 23 | 27 | $67 |
2183 W. 4th Ave. (bet. Arbutus & Yew Sts.), 604-738-2025;
www.bishopsonline.com
Thanks to the "sincerity and warmth" of "unsurpassed host" John
Bishop and his "amazing" team of professionals, this "intimate"
West Side "classic" ranks No. 1 for Service in the *Vancouver
Survey*; the kitchen, too, is "brilliant", using mostly "organic
ingredients" to prepare "top-of-the-line" fare that reflects the
"Pacific Northwest at its best"; "save your pennies for a splurge"
at this "perennial favourite."

Bistro Pastis   25 | 21 | 23 | $53 |
2153 W. 4th Ave. (bet. Arbutus & Yew Sts.), 604-731-5020;
www.pastis.ca
"First-class French country fare" at comparatively "reasonable
prices", combined with "attentive service" headed by "hands-
on" owner John Blakeley, make this West Sider all that an "authentic" "neighbourhood bistro should be"; start with a pastis,
then move on to "to-die-for" coq au vin at a "cosseting", "local"
spot "where everyone goes for comfort."

Blue Water Cafe & Raw Bar ☽   25 | 24 | 22 | $57 |
1095 Hamilton St. (Helmcken St.), 604-688-8078;
www.bluewatercafe.net
"The fish are still flopping just before they reach your table" at this
"bustling" seafood "hot spot" in a "trendy Yaletown" warehouse,
where the "top-notch raw bar", "amazing tower" of crustaceans
and "innovative" sushi are a "religious experience"; the "service
is accommodating" – if you "dress to impress" – and "celeb-
sighting" abounds, but some say prices "leave them blue."

___

Brix ◗🅰   21 | 22 | 20 | $45
1138 Homer St. (bet. Davie & Helmcken Sts.), 604-915-9463;
www.brixvancouver.com
Built around the "fantastic courtyard" of a 1912 heritage building,
this Pacific Northwester in Yaletown lets diners linger till 2 AM
over "good small plates" and "great martinis"; the "relaxed atmosphere" makes it "fun with a group or date."

Café de Paris   21 | 18 | 19 | $48
751 Denman St. (bet. Alberni & Robson Sts.), 604-687-1418
"When the Visa balance won't allow a fast escape to the
Marais", diners visit this "enchanting" West Ender serving "classic" bistro mainstays to get "as close to France as they can get";
the "welcoming service" in this "reliable" "standby" helps offset
quarters that, *bien sûr*, are a little "cramped."

Cafe Il Nido 🅰   21 | 18 | 21 | $48
780 Thurlow St. (Robson St.), 604-685-6436;
www.cafeilnido.net
Fans are a-flutter over this "intimate" Downtowner serving "consistent" Italian fare in a "quiet" room "nestled away" off Robson
Street; the decor may be "dated", but the "tasty" dishes "more
than make up for it", and as chef-owner Franco Felice is one of the
"nicest hosts you could meet", "the whole experience is worth it."

Caffe de Medici   25 | 23 | 27 | $50
109-1025 Robson St. (bet. Burrard & Thurlow Sts.), 604-669-9322;
www.caffedemedici.com
Known for "memorable" plates of "hearty", "traditional" fare,
paired with "spectacular" wines, this "stylish", "little secret" in a
"cosy nook on bustling Robson" has been "dependable" for
"high-quality Italian dining" since 1979; "fabulous service" from
a "knowledgeable staff" helps create "a delightful evening" for
regulars and "European guests" alike.

Cannery, The   24 | 23 | 23 | $51
2205 Commissioner St. (Victoria Dr.), 604-254-9606;
www.canneryseafood.com
"Sit by the windows" overlooking "Canada's busiest harbour"
and let the "great staff" tempt you with "delicious", "traditional"
seafood at this "old-school" East Sider "hidden" "between working wharves"; it's a "long-time favourite" "to take visitors" (so, of

course, it's "touristy") – just "bring a map", as locating it can be "like finding a needle in a haystack."

Cardero's Restaurant & Marine Pub ◑ 20 | 23 | 21 | $40
1583 Coal Harbour Quay (bet. Cardero & Nicola Sts.),
604-669-7666
"It's always hopping" at this "boisterous" West End "roadhouse on stilts" that packs 'em in for "beautiful" Coal Harbour vistas; "attentive" service from the "attractive staff" makes this a "wonderful place to meet up with friends after a hard day's work" where the "above-average view" trumps the "average", "upscale pub food."

Cassis Bistro ◑ 20 | 17 | 18 | $34
420 W. Pender St. (bet. Homer & Richards Sts.), 604-605-0420;
www.cassisvancouver.com
"Kick back, hang out and enjoy" the "authentic French peasant food" at this "amazing value" Downtown, where "small portions at small prices" draw an "interesting mix of customers"; though the "comfort" fare "can use a notch of improvement" and the service is "a little scattered", this "casual bistro" with soaring ceilings "mostly hits its marks"; P.S. there's entertainment on many nights.

Century – | – | – | E
432 Richards St. (bet. W. Hastings & W. Pender Sts.),
604-633-2700
Amid giant murals of cowboys and Che Guevara, this elegantly funky Downtowner in a sumptuously furnished former bank delivers Nuevo Latino cuisine with flair; settle into a cushy leather booth and sip mojitos or other creative cocktails before sampling Dungeness crab burritos or paella.

Chambar Belgian Restaurant 25 | 24 | 21 | $47
562 Beatty St. (bet. Dunsmuir & W. Pender Sts.), 604-879-7119;
www.chambar.com
"Raves all around" for this "happening", brick-lined "room with a great buzz", a "fantastic addition" to Downtown; chef Nico Schuermans' "oh-so-tender lamb" and other "fabulous" Belgian-inspired fare pull in "pretty people", as do the "amazing" beer list and "brilliant" cocktails, while a staff that's "exceptional (without being overwhelming)" helps the "high-energy" space feel both "hip and welcoming."

Chartwell 25 | 25 | 27 | $71
Four Seasons Hotel, 791 W. Georgia St. (Howe St.), 604-844-6715;
www.fourseasons.com
"Everything proper in the Four Seasons tradition" makes this
"clubby" Downtowner "the grande dame of Vancouver dining"; the
staff delivers "superb" service in a "formal" room with a "big fireplace", and the Pacific Northwest fare is "delightfully delicious";
it's "pricey", but for a "special occasion", it's "exquisite."

Ch'i Restaurant & Lounge ⬤ ∇ 27 | 24 | 25 | $41
1796 Nanaimo St. (E. 1st Ave.), 604-215-0078; www.chirestaurant.ca
"Hidden amongst gas stations and cheap take-out joints", this
"deep–East Side find" has insiders cheering the "culinary de-
lights" of the "innovative" Pacific Northwest–meets-Asia "tapas
treats", including kimchi mussels and pan-seared duck breast;
"ambiance to kill" and a staff that "really seems to know the
food" have helped the "classy" joint "raise the bar" in the area.

CINCIN RISTORANTE 23 | 23 | 22 | $52
1154 Robson St. (bet. Bute & Thurlow Sts.), 604-688-7338; www.cincin.net
A "sexy place" "for a first date" that's also "popular with tourists,
business types" and "Hollywood North", this "beautiful retreat"
above "the Robson Street craziness" is "on almost everyone's hit
parade"; from the "rich flavours" of the "rustic" Med fare to the
"courteous", "darkly clad" staff delivering "service with a smile"
amid the "glitterati", it's always "satisfying" for a "lively" evening.

CIOPPINO'S MEDITERRANEAN GRILL 🖾 26 | 23 | 25 | $65
1133 Hamilton St. (bet. Davie & Helmcken Sts.), 604-688-7466;
www.cioppinosyaletown.com
"Brilliant" chef-owner Pino Posteraro "turns out amazing"
Mediterranean dishes from the "open kitchen" of his "outstanding" Yaletowner, run by a "helpful staff"; it's a "fine destination for
wine weenies" – the "serious list" includes 1,300+ bottles – and
while it's "not inexpensive", *amici* aver that this "epitome of sublime cuisine and service" is "one of the town's best."

Circolo 🖾 24 | 25 | 23 | $59
1116 Mainland St. (bet. Davie & Helmcken Sts.), 604-687-1116;
www.umberto.com
"Power brokers" mix with "romantics" on the garden patio or in
the dark-wood interior near the nightly piano player to sup on

osso bucco and other "classic Italian" fare at this Yaletowner; though a few fuss that it's "nice but never excellent", most maintain it's "another success" for prolific restaurateur Umberto Menghi.

Coast ●   23 | 25 | 23 | $57
1257 Hamilton St. (bet. Davie & Drake Sts.), 604-685-5010;
www.coastrestaurant.ca
Gourmet groupies "wear black" and "interact" with the "cool crowd" at the "convivial" "community table" at this "upscale" eatery that's "heavy on the Yaletown vibe"; even agoraphobes agree that the "creative choices" on the "inventive" seafood menu "satisfy" in a "chic" space that feels like you're "eating in a *Dwell Magazine* photo spread."

C RESTAURANT   26 | 24 | 26 | $67
2-1600 Howe St. (Beach Ave.), 604-681-1164; www.crestaurant.com
"The passion shows" affirm fin-atics of "wildly innovative" chef Robert Clark's "superlative seafood", "superbly presented" and "expertly served" in a "stylish", "stunning" "waterfront setting" Downtown overlooking False Creek; environmentalists applaud the spot's "eco-friendly" support for "sustainable fishing practices", and everyone agrees that, while you'll "C your wallet shrink" ("the prices are unbelievably high"), it's a "must-visit."

Cru   26 | 21 | 24 | $51
1459 W. Broadway (bet. Granville & Hemlock Sts.), 604-677-4111;
www.cru.ca
Oenophiles appreciate the "unique, colour-coded" list of "scrumptious wines" that match with "fantastic" Pacific Northwest "plates to share" or one of the "best prix fixes in the city" at this "intimate" West Side bistro; though the storefront is "small" and "minimalist", a grape-savvy staff that encourages you to "try something new" "without a bit of snobbery" at "relatively affordable prices" "allows you to be a regular."

Delilah's ●   22 | 22 | 23 | $47
1789 Comox St. (Denman St.), 604-687-3424; www.delilahs.ca
"Martinis galore" are "the highlight" at this "sexy", "irreverent" "place to celebrate anything worth celebrating"; the "charmingly" "camp" staff "caters to the fabulous eccentricities of the West End", serving up "competent" Pacific Northwest fare to "diverse locals" and "visiting celebs", making for a "blast."

Diner ∉   ▽ 20 | 14 | 10 | $26
1269 Hamilton St. (bet. Davie & Drake Sts.), 604-444-4855
"Delish desserts" headline the menu of "home-style" "comfort
food" at this Eclectic Yaletown diner by toque-owner Heather
Clark, formerly an assistant pastry chef at New York's Jean
Georges; "the portions are substantial" and "the value is terrific",
but with service that's "beyond slow", you may have to "block off
half your day for a meal."

Diva at the Met   26 | 23 | 25 | $61
*Metropolitan Hotel, 645 Howe St. (bet. Dunsmuir & W. Georgia Sts.),
604-602-7788; www.metropolitan.com*
At lunch when "deals are made", "prior to the opera" or "for a
splurge night", this Downtown "delectable diva" draws ovations
for "beautifully plated" Pacific Northwest dishes and "orgasmic
desserts" by chocolatier Thomas Haas; "prepare to be impressed"
by the "witty staff" in this "airy" space, particularly if you sit near
"the open kitchen" to watch the "chefs work their magic."

Don Francesco Ristorante   24 | 18 | 24 | $49
*860 Burrard St. (bet. Robson & Smithe Sts.), 604-685-7770;
www.donfrancesco.ca*
"Old-world charm and sophistication abound" at this Downtown
Italian noted for its "luscious" fare and for the namesake owner's
propensity to "break out in a personal operatic serenade"; the
"personable staff" contributes to an "enjoyable" evening that
"won't bankrupt you."

EN Japanese Restaurant ⊠   24 | 17 | 19 | $40
2686 Granville St. (bet. W. 10th & 11th Aves.), 604-730-0330
"Vancouver's best-kept secret for modern Japanese" may be this
spare West Side room where the "creative fusion" fare can
"amaze the palate"; perhaps service "can be slow" because so
"much care is taken in the presentation" – cognoscenti concur
that "if this were New York, it would command the same esteem
as Nobu", at "a quarter of the price."

Feenie's ◐   24 | 22 | 21 | $45
*2563 W. Broadway (bet. Larch & Trafalgar Sts.), 604-739-7115;
www.feenies.com*
"Beautiful" "Kitsilano hipsters" and "rich yuppies wanting burgers" and other "gourmet takes" on Pacific Northwest fare "run"

to this "cutting-edge" "casual" "sib to high-end Lumière"; the employees "look as good as the food" – and the "flashy" "red room makes everyone appear to be fabulous" – but the "über-cool attitude" is a turnoff for those who find this West Sider "too trendy."

Fiddlehead Joe's 20 | 20 | 20 | $34
1012 Beach Ave. (Hornby St.), 604-688-1969;
www.fiddleheadjoeseatery.com
A "perfect place to watch the world walk by" or see "the roller-bladers stumble" is this Downtowner "perched on the seawall"; "brunch on a sunny weekend is ideal", and the casual Pacific Northwest cuisine is "yummy for dinner", though oglers opine that "the food can't help but be overpowered" by the "fantastic" False Creek views.

Fish House in Stanley Park 22 | 22 | 21 | $47
8901 Stanley Park Dr. (Beach Ave.), 604-681-7275;
www.fishhousestanleypark.com
For "fresh seafood" "simply" and "carefully prepared", fin fans "take a cab" or "stroll through Stanley Park" to this "charming" West Ender that's "lovely" for a "leisurely meal"; afishionados lured by "local cooking celeb" Karen Barnaby's low-carb options also salute the "proper staff" and "relatively reasonable prices."

Five Sails 25 | 26 | 26 | $69
Pan Pacific Hotel, 300-999 Canada Pl. (Howe St.), 604-891-2892;
www.dinepanpacific.com
"Breathtaking vistas over the harbour" and "white-glove service" lend a "romantic aura" to this "formal" Pan Pacific Hotel Downtowner; the "creative" French-influenced Pacific Northwest fare is "beautifully prepared and presented", and the "amazing wine list" reads "like a novel", so "go on your anniversary or birthday" – just "be prepared to flex your credit card limits."

Fleuri 24 | 22 | 25 | $59
Sutton Place Hotel, 845 Burrard St. (bet. Robson & Smithe Sts.), 604-642-2900; www.suttonplace.com
"Movie celebs" frequent this "high-quality" room in the Sutton Place Hotel Downtown, where the "elegant French food" and "impeccable service" mean you "eat as well as any millionaire"; the chocolate buffet Thursday, Friday and Saturday evenings is so "unbelievable", it "should be illegal."

Globe @ YVR
21 | 21 | 22 | $45

*Fairmont Vancouver Airport Hotel, 3111 North Service Rd.
(off Grant McConachie Way), Richmond, 604-207-5200*

"Get a window seat" and "eat prior to your flight (or just because
you like to watch planes)" at this "upscale" Vancouver
International eatery that serves "delicious" Pacific Northwest
fare with "a fascinating runway view"; the staff is "exceptionally
helpful", so frequent fliers agree that this "soundproofed" oasis
is "the best airport" restaurant "to get stranded in"; P.S. it's also
"worth lingering" in the "high-tech" lounge.

glowbal grill & satay bar ◐
22 | 23 | 21 | $44

*1079 Mainland St. (bet. Helmcken & Nelson Sts.), 604-602-0835;
www.glowbalgrill.com*

"Beautiful people" flock to this "vibrant" Yaletown hot spot
for "delicious" Eclectic fare, including "more than great satay";
the "funky, mod decor" lends it an "urban-chic ambiance"
that "crackles with electricity" (maybe that's why it's so "loud"),
while an "attentive staff" "gives the royal treatment" to an "oh-
so-trendy" crowd; the AFTERglow lounge is "a great place to
end the night."

Go Fish!
25 | 15 | 16 | $17

1505 W. 1st Ave. (Fisherman's Wharf), 604-730-5040

"The fish is delish" at this "tin shack" at the docks near Granville
Island, where the "divine" seafood comes "right off the boats";
owner Gord Martin (Bin 941, Bin 942) has created an "easy-on-
the-wallet" "alfresco lunch" spot that's "perfect" "on a sunny
day", though it's the "shivering customers eating outside in
midwinter" who demonstrate the true "popularity of this gem."

Gotham Steakhouse
26 | 25 | 24 | $65

*615 Seymour St. (bet. Dunsmuir & W. Georgia Sts.), 604-605-8282;
www.gothamsteakhouse.com*

"Wear a power suit" and "impress your carnivore friends" with
"the best steak in the city" at this "top-notch" Downtown chophouse boasting the "gorgeous vaulted ceilings" and "dark
leather" interior "you'd expect" from "old-school" "fine dining";
the "knowledgeable" servers treat you like you "belong to a pri-
vate club", but with the à la carte pricing ("which means 'no po-
tato' in French"), you might hope that "someone else is picking
up the tab."

Griffins Restaurant   21 | 20 | 21 | $43
Fairmont Hotel Vancouver, 900 W. Georgia St. (Burrard St.),
604-662-1900; www.fairmonthotel.com
Belly up to the "high-quality" smorgasbord in this "stately room"
at the "elegant" Fairmont Hotel Vancouver Downtown (where
you can also "order from the menu" of Pacific Northwest fare);
the staff "treats regulars like family", the better to "impress visiting relatives" – just tell your uncle to "save room" for the
"scrumptious" "all-you-can-eat dessert bar."

Gyoza King ◑   24 | 13 | 16 | $22
1508 Robson St. (bet. Cardero & Nicola Sts.), 604-669-8278
"Amazing gyoza, duh!" proclaim "worshipers at the dumpling al-
tar" of this "budget-friendly" West End "hole-in-the-wall" for
Japanese tapas; "expect lineups" of "exchange students" and
"hit-or-miss service", but know that at this "cheap", "cheerful" "di-
version from all the generic sushi places", you'll "eat like a king."

Habibi's ☒   21 | 12 | 20 | $21
1128 W. Broadway (bet. Oak & Spruce Sts.), 604-732-7487;
www.habibis.com
Even "carnivores never feel deprived" at this Lebanese vegetarian in a "basic" West Side storefront, where the "delicious vari-
ety" is "so tasty you forget it's also healthy"; the "addicted"
"order one of everything and share with friends", and the easy
"prices and friendly service" "keep them coming back."

Habit Lounge ◑   ∇ 22 | 25 | 25 | $30
2610 Main St. (bet. E. 10th & 11th Aves.), 604-877-8582;
www.habitlounge.ca
Already "hopping", this "great new addition" to the East Side's
South Main area is a "low-lit den of hipness" done up with "spun
plastic lamps, orange vinyl and antlers"; habitués "there to soci-
alise" over "yummy" Eclectic "share plates" say there may be
"kinks to work out", but the staff "knows what they're doing."

Hapa Izakaya ◑   22 | 20 | 19 | $36
1479 Robson St. (bet. Broughton & Nicola Sts.), 604-689-4272
The "'in' crowd" "packs" this "hip Japanese pub" in the West End
"to share" "tasty" small plates or to "sit at the bar and enjoy" the
"great vibe"; a staff that "welcomes you with a shout and a smile"
suggests this "stylish room" "could be renamed Happy Izakaya."

Hart House, The   22 | 22 | 23 | $46
6664 Deer Lake Ave. (bet. Canada Way & Sperling Ave.), Burnaby,
604-298-4278; www.harthouserestaurant.com
"A step back in time", this "inviting" heritage house with a "beautiful view" of Deer Lake in Burnaby offers "well-presented" Pacific Northwest fare and "classic" service; diners who come "for a nice, quiet dinner" where they are treated "like old friends" say that it's a "quaint" escape from "the hustle and bustle."

Hermitage, The   23 | 20 | 23 | $55
115-1025 Robson St. (bet. Burrard & Thurlow Sts.), 604-689-3237;
www.thehermitagevancouver.com
Proving that "formal, friendly service is not a contradiction in terms", chef-owner Hervé Martin and his staff "make customers feel welcome" at this "oldie but goodie" on Robson; a "loyal following" finds "excellent" French fare paired with "wine from the family château" in Burgundy, shrugging off modernists who maintain it's "a throwback."

Herons   23 | 22 | 24 | $55
Fairmont Waterfront Hotel, 900 Canada Place Way (bet. Burrard &
Howe Sts.), 604-691-1818; www.fairmont.com
The "beautiful" view out the floor-to-ceiling windows is as expansive as the all-you-can-eat buffets at this Pacific Northwester in the Fairmont Waterfront Downtown that pairs a "great atmosphere" and "excellent service" with "wonderful" "regional foods"; there's also "easy access to the cruise dock and convention centre."

Horizons on Burnaby Mountain   21 | 24 | 22 | $44
100 Centennial Way (Burnaby Mtn. Park), Burnaby, 604-299-1155;
www.horizonsrestaurant.com
"On a clear day" you can "see all of Downtown" from this "beautiful" room atop Burnaby Mountain; "the service is quite good" too, which makes it "a great place to impress a date" or "dazzle visitors from out of town", though the competent Pacific Northwest cuisine may "play second fiddle" to the "breathtaking" setting.

Hy's Encore   23 | 20 | 23 | $59
637 Hornby St. (bet. Dunsmuir & W. Georgia Sts.), 604-683-7671;
www.hyssteakhouse.com
Its "dark, red velvet" interior, "many of the staff" "and even the crumpled foil on the cheese bread" seemingly "haven't changed

in 40 years" at this "classic" Downtown steakhouse boasting "flame-grilled" beef and "impeccable" service; "this classy old joint full of classy old people" "hasn't gone trendy", and Hy-stakes players like it that way.

IL GIARDINO DI UMBERTO ⊠   26 24 25 $60
1382 Hornby St. (Pacific St.), 604-669-2422; www.umberto.com
Some of "the best Italian fare" is served in this "rustic yet regal" Tuscan-style "period house" Downtown that's "romantic" enough "for any intimate celebration"; owner Umberto Menghi ("Vancouver's Wolfgang Puck") presides over a "power patio" that makes for "good beautiful-people viewing" at a "little gem" that's all about "consistent" "fine dining" and "warm hospitality"; N.B. a scheduled fall 2006 redo may outdate the Decor score and lead to a temporary closing.

Imperial Chinese Seafood   24 21 19 $39
355 Burrard St. (W. Hastings St.), 604-688-8191; www.imperialrest.com
"Dress up for" "delicious dim sum", seafood so "fresh" "you'd think the fisherman had his boat tied up outside" and other "excellent Cantonese" at Vancouver's "most elegant Chinese" in the "stunning" Marine Building Downtown; its "high ceilings" and "two-storey windows" yield "picturesque" views, so though "you almost have to beg for service", most "would return tomorrow."

Joe Fortes   21 21 22 $50
777 Thurlow St. (bet. Alberni & Robson Sts.), 604-669-1940;
www.joefortes.ca
Bivalvists bet on this "lively" "American-style" surf 'n' turfer Downtown for its "impressive oyster bar's" "fresh, regional" shellfish and for other "simply prepared" "classics" served by a "professional" team; the "rooftop bar's" "upbeat" scene "rocks" "in the summer", despite dissenters who dub this "longtime landmark" too "predictable."

Kalamata Greek Taverna   21 13 19 $26
478 W. Broadway (bet. Cambie & Yukon Sts.), 604-872-7050
"Like an old friend", this West Side "mainstay" serves "generous portions" of "good, reliable Greek food"; cravers of the signature *kleftiko* commend this "lamb shoulder to die for", though no one extends an olive branch to a space that "desperately needs to be spruced up."

KEG STEAKHOUSE & BAR, THE   20 | 18 | 20 | $38
1499 Anderson St. (bet. Duranleau & Johnston Sts.), 604-685-4735 ◐
595 Hornby St. (Dunsmuir St.), 604-687-4044 ◐
742 Thurlow St. (bet. Alberni & Robson Sts.), 604-685-4388 ◐
2656 Eastbrook Pkwy. (Stillcreek Ave.), Burnaby, 604-294-4626 ◐
6913 120th St. (72nd Ave.), Delta, 604-591-6161
800 Columbia St. (8th St.), New Westminster, 604-524-1381
11151 No. 5 Rd. (bet. Horseshoe Way & Steveston Hwy.),
Richmond, 604-272-1399
15146 100th Ave. (152nd St.), Surrey, 604-583-6700 ◐
Park Royal South Mall, 800 Marine Dr. (Taylor Way),
West Vancouver, 604-925-9126 ◐
www.kegsteakhouse.com
"You can always count" on "good steak with all the fixin's" at this "reasonably priced" chophouse chain, where the "energetic staff" is "expert at getting crowds seated" and "promptly" served; "catch a game at the bar" or "bring the family" ("don't let the frat-boy name fool you" – they're "attentive to kids"), though you might want to leave "your foodie friends" home.

Kirin Mandarin   25 | 17 | 21 | $40
1166 Alberni St. (bet. Bute & Thurlow Sts.), 604-682-8833;
www.kirinrestaurant.com
"Authentic" Northern Chinese fare, including "Peking duck that can't be beat" and "fresh seafood" fished live from the tanks, attracts Sinophiles to this "elegant Asian" Downtown for "big, banquet-style dinners" or business lunches; "dim sum is always a treat," brought by a "knowledgeable, helpful staff."

Kirin Seafood   23 | 20 | 19 | $37
City Sq., 555 W. 12th Ave., 2nd fl. (Cambie St.), 604-879-8038
Henderson Pl., 1163 Pinetree Way (bet. Glen Dr. & Lincoln Ave.),
Coquitlam, 604-944-8833
Three West Ctr., 7900 Westminster Hwy., 2nd fl. (bet. Minoru Blvd. &
No. 3 Rd.), Richmond, 604-303-8833
www.kirinrestaurant.com
The "seafood is amazing" and the dim sum "top-notch" at this "authentic" Cantonese trio on the West Side, in Richmond and Coquitlam; admirers who appreciate the "extensive menu" and "attentive service" advise "go with more people to order more dishes" at this "perfect place for family" events.

Kitanoya Guu ◗   25 | 19 | 20 | $25
838 Thurlow St. (bet. Robson & Smithe Sts.), 604-685-8817
Kitanoya Guu with Garlic ◗
1698 Robson St. (Bidwell St.), 604-685-8678
Kitanoya Guu with Otokamae ◗
105-375 Water St. (W. Cordova St.), 604-685-8682
"Unbelievably good", "shockingly cheap" "small dishes with big
tastes" are the hallmark of this "chaotic" Japanese *izakaya* trio
"transported" to Downtown, where the "lively staff hollers your
order across the packed restaurant"; "you might have to wait, but
it's worth it" for this "unique" experience that's popular with the
"young and hip" – despite "the hearing loss you may suffer."

Kobe Japanese Steak House ◗   23 | 19 | 23 | $48
1042 Alberni St. (bet. Burrard & Thurlow Sts.), 604-684-2451;
www.koberestaurant.com
Your chefs "toss their knives" as they cook teppanyaki-style "at
your table" at this Downtown Japanese steakhouse that "enter-
tains" "those who have never experienced this kind of dining
spectacle"; the beef is "done perfectly", and foodies who frown
upon the "fun, rather than gourmet", fare and the "tired" setting
admit it might "impress" "visitors who get squeamish at sushi."

La Belle Auberge   ▽ 28 | 22 | 26 | $65
4856 48th Ave. (48 B St.), Ladner, 604-946-7717;
www.labelleauberge.com
The "award-winning" menu by chef-owner Bruno Marti goes for
gold with "classic, yet innovative French fare" served in a
"charming" 1905 heritage house that's "off the beaten track" in
bucolic Ladner; while it's "not cheap", the "excellent" *table
d'hôte* or "special splurge" options like kangaroo fillet with red
currants and brandy cream make it "a gourmet's must."

LA REGALADE ⌧   27 | 19 | 25 | $52
102-2232 Marine Dr. (bet. 22nd & 23rd Sts.), West Vancouver,
604-921-2228; www.laregalade.com
"*C'est magnifique*" rave regulars who "adore *la cuisine
française*" at this "mighty authentic" West Vancouver bistro
that's "well worth the trip over a bridge – any bridge" to tuck into
"ample portions" of "heartwarming" "French country" fare "me-
ticulously prepared" by chef-owner Alain Rayé; the "quarters are
close", but it's "like finding yourself in France."

La Terrazza   22 | 23 | 22 | $52

1088 Cambie St. (Pacific Blvd.), 604-899-4449; www.laterrazza.ca
This "elegant" Yaletowner has a "wonderful ambiance" "in
which to be pampered" over "fresh, interesting Italian dishes"
paired with wines from the "extensive list" of 2,000+ bottles;
oenophiles watch for "special tasting nights" with prix fixe
menus and "suitably matching" vino.

LE CROCODILE ⌧   27 | 23 | 26 | $67

100-909 Burrard St. (Smithe St.), 604-669-4298;
www.lecrocodilerestaurant.com
"Are we in France?" clientele query chef-owner Michel Jacob,
an "Alsatian prince" whose "sublime" cuisine bears the "Gallic
consistency of a master"; there are "no crocodile tears" shed in
this "stylish" Downtown "oasis" where the "discreet" staff
"spoils" you (and the diners, *bien sûr*, are "expected to behave"),
so whether "for a civilised lunch or a romantic evening", it is
"worth every penny."

LIFT   19 | 27 | 19 | $54

333 Menchions Mews (Bay Shore Dr.), 604-689-5438;
www.liftbarandgrill.com
"Who cares what they're serving" at this "stunning" Pacific
Northwester, since "it's hip, hot" and boasts a "knockout design" in
a "spectacular" West End waterfront setting?; too bad the staff can
be "desultory (unless you look like you walked off a movie set)" say
sightseers who also suggest raising the "pedestrian" plates "to
the standard of the location" – right on the Coal Harbour seawall.

Lolita's South of the Border Cantina ● ▽ 22 | 18 | 19 | $34

1326 Davie St. (bet. Broughton & Jervis Sts.), 604-696-9996
"At last", cry compadres cheering the arrival of this "surprising
oasis of tequila in the West End"; besides being a "happening"
new "neighborhood haunt" for hooch, it serves up "authentic",
"creative" Mexican fare, so despite "cramped quarters", enthusiasts exclaim "long may the fiesta continue!"

Lombardo's Ristorante   24 | 13 | 19 | $22

Il Mercato, 120-1641 Commercial Dr. (E. 1st Ave.), 604-251-2240;
www.lombardospizzeria.com
Don't let the setting in an "odd shopping mall" "deter you" – some
of "the best thin-crust pizzas" come out of the "wood-fired ovens"

of this East Side Italian that also serves "perfectly al dente pasta"
and "fresh, well-portioned salads"; "friendly service" and "down-
to-earth pricing" round out the reasons why it's a "looks-can-be-
deceiving winner"; N.B. a new branch is slated for Downtown.

LUMIÈRE
28 | 24 | 26 | $105

*2551 W. Broadway (bet. Larch & Trafalgar Sts.), 604-739-8185;
www.lumiere.ca*
"Breathtaking in its simplicity", with "fabulous tasting menus"
"showcasing local purveyors", chef Rob Feenie's "awesome"
French fare is a "serious gourmand experience" that rates as the
Vancouver Survey's Most Popular; "special-occasion" pilgrims
to this candlelit West Side room revere the "decadent parade" of
"well-planned courses" brought by a "superb" (if "pretentious")
staff; those who "love every bite" but flinch at a meal "on par with
a mortgage" dine in the adjacent Tasting Bar for "a steal."

Marcello
21 | 18 | 14 | $27

1404 Commercial Dr. (Kitchener St.), 604-215-7760
"Terrific pizza" (from the sun-god-shaped "wood-burning oven")
and "great pasta" create "lineups" at this "friendly" East Side
Italian, set in a "loud", "lively" "cavernous space"; bring "the
kids" "for an inexpensive meal" topped off by "*tiramisu* to die for."

Maurya Indian Cuisine
20 | 24 | 21 | $38

*1643 W. Broadway (bet. Fir & Pine Sts.), 604-742-0622;
www.mauryaindiancuisine.com*
A "stunning design" of "opulent" woods, high ceilings and over-
size windows creates a "dramatic ambiance" at this "classy"
West Side Indian; the weekday lunch buffet is "a bargain", and
the staff "caters" to guests' needs while serving "well-executed,
traditional" fare, even if spice-hounds bark about "high-priced",
"toned-down" dishes.

Memphis Blues Barbeque House
23 | 12 | 15 | $22

*1342 Commercial Dr. (bet. Charles & Kitchener Sts.), 604-215-2599
1465 W. Broadway (bet. Granville & Hemlock Sts.), 604-738-6806
www.memphisbluesbbq.com*
"Vegetarians, stay home!" admonish admirers of these East and
West Side "carnivals for carnivores"; "gut-busting portions" of
"superb ribs", "fabulous brisket" and "great beans and slaw"
make this BBQ duo "worthy of the Memphis name", though ser-

vice can be "surly" and both the "uninspired space" and "killer
waits" suggest "takeout is the way to go."

Mistral Bistro 　　24 | 18 | 24 | $48
*2585 W. Broadway (bet. Larch & Trafalgar Sts.), 604-733-0046;
www.mistralbistro.ca*
"Foodies longing for a trip to France" are blown away by this
"classic Gallic bistro" on the West Side that's "run by a delightful,
hardworking" couple; Jean-Yves Benoît prepares "outstanding"
fare like "comforting cassoulet" at "reasonable prices", while his
wife, Minna, leads a "cosseting" staff at this "newcomer" that "ups
the stakes in the race for French supremacy" in Vancouver.

Montri's Thai　　24 | 15 | 20 | $33
*3629 W. Broadway (bet. Alma & Dunbar Sts.), 604-738-9888;
www.montri-thai.com*
"Year in and year out", the "best Thai food in town", say fans,
comes from this "small" West Sider known for "warmth on the
plate and in the room"; "affable" chef-owner Montri Rattanaraj
creates "delicate flavours, spiced right", and his "congenial"
staff's "knowledgeable approach to wine" helps make for
a "Thai-rrific" experience.

Morton's, The Steakhouse　　25 | 22 | 25 | $68
*750 W. Cordova St. (bet. Granville & Howe Sts.), 604-915-5105;
www.mortons.com*
"Order your meat rare and your drinks stiff" advise patrons of this
"upscale American chain outpost" Downtown noted for its "flavourful" steaks of "monolithic proportions" served in an "old-
boys'-club atmosphere"; just "pack your wallet" – this "classy"
experience doesn't come cheap.

Nat's New York Pizzeria　　21 | 11 | 18 | $12
*1080 Denman St. (bet. Comox & Pendrell Sts.), 604-642-0777
2684 W. Broadway (bet. Stephens & Trafalgar Sts.), 604-737-0707
www.natspizza.com*
It's "Brooklyn with a Canadian accent" at these "cheap, delicious"
"New York–style" pizzerias, the No. 1 Bang for the Buck in the
Vancouver Survey; though the wisecracking, "people-friendly"
staffers "are the decor" at the bare-bones West Side/West End
duo, regulars "keep them on speed dial" for "thin-crust pies"
made "with top-quality ingredients."

Nu ◑   22 | 20 | 22 | $50

1661 Granville St. (Pacific St.), 604-646-4668; www.whatisnu.com

"Like a Holland America flashback", this "groovy" "new winner" has a "smashing retro design" and a "cool" seawall setting Downtown, though no "cruise-ship lounge" ever served such "cutting-edge" Eclectic fare; "trendy" tasters who "love the cocktails" and the "innovative" tapas also applaud the "charming staff" but whine what's with those "uncomfortable chairs"?

Ocean 6 Seventeen   – | – | – | E

617 Stamp's Landing (off Moberly Rd.), 604-879-6178; www.ocean617.com

It's "well worth the trip" to this "cute" eatery with an "obscure location" "tucked away in Stamp's Landing"; the few surveyors who've discovered the "great little waterfront" bistro sample "excellent" Pacific Northwest fare and affordable wines brought by the "attentive staff", while "enjoying" the False Creek views.

O'Doul's Restaurant & Bar   21 | 19 | 21 | $37

Listel Hotel, 1300 Robson St. (Jervis St.), 604-661-1400;
www.odoulsrestaurant.com

"There's nothing Irish about this" "relaxing oasis" in the West End's Listel Hotel, where "the servers know their stuff" and nightly jazz is "an added bonus"; Pacific Northwest dishes include "something for everyone", from "no-frills" steak to the "decent" weekend brunch, though some warble that the food "doesn't hit any high notes."

Pajo's ⊭   24 | 13 | 18 | $13

Rocky Point Park, 2800 Murray St. (Moody St.), Port Moody, 604-469-2289
Garry Point Park (Chatham St.), Richmond, 604-204-0767
The Wharf, Bayview & Third Sts. (waterfront), Richmond, 604-272-1588
Boundary Bay Regional Park, 600 Centennial Pkwy. (Hwy. 17),
Tsawwassen, 604-943-7930
www.pajos.com

Prepare to "fight off seagulls to keep" the "crispy", "fantastically fresh", "English-style" fish 'n' chips "to yourself" at this "great-value" seasonal seafood quartet; "you'll wait in line", but on a "sunny day" with "marvelous scenery", "who could ask for more?"

Parkside   25 | 23 | 25 | $53

1906 Haro St. (Gilford St.), 604-683-6912; www.parksiderestaurant.ca

"Mouth orgasms" – that's what smitten surveyors call chef-owner Andrey Durbach's "seasonally changing" Modern

European inventions, made with "the freshest ingredients" and served prix fixe for "one of the best deals in town"; the staff is "attentive but not hovering" at this "intimate" West End "hideaway" where, from "succulent cocktails" to "delicious desserts", a "brilliant" meal leaves you "feeling happy-happy."

PEAR TREE, THE 🗷   28 | 22 | 27 | $57

4120 E. Hastings St. (bet. Carleton & Gilmore Aves.), Burnaby, 604-299-2772

At this "sophisticated", "welcome find in the culinary desert of Burnaby", "one of the country's top talents", chef-owner Scott Jaeger, puts out "fabulous", "imaginative" Continental plates; co-owner Stephanie Jaeger heads up a "stellar front-of-house" team, and "recent renovations have added a high-end touch" to the "small" but "charming" room.

Pink Pearl Chinese Seafood   22 | 11 | 16 | $26

1132 E. Hastings St. (bet. Clark & Vernon Drs.), 604-253-4316; www.pinkpearl.com

"Dim sum is the way to go" at this "hangar-sized" East Sider known for "scrumptious", "inexpensive" small plates "served the old-fashioned way" as "trolley after trolley whizzes past your table"; "all walks of life are leveled by their need for dumplings" here, even as detractors declare the place has been surpassed "by newer and glitzier Chinese palaces" with not-quite-so-"surly" staff.

Provence Marinaside   21 | 21 | 20 | $46

1177 Marinaside Cres. (bet. Aquarius Mews & Davie St.), 604-681-4144; www.provencevancouver.com

The chilled seafood platter, "delectable antipasti" and "top-of-the-list" Sunday brunch make up the "winning combination" of French fare that lures fans to this Yaletown seawall eatery; the staff is "attentive" and the room is "cosy", but "when the weather is performing well", the biggest draw is the "remarkable setting."

Provence Mediterranean Grill   22 | 19 | 21 | $46

4473 W. 10th Ave. (bet. Sasamat & Trimble Sts.), 604-222-1980; www.provencevancouver.com

For a "relaxed meal", this "unpretentious but upscale" West Side "favourite" serves "flavourful" French-Med fare; an "efficient" staff manages the "lovely" room, and at least on a day when there's "sun instead of rain", you'll feel like you're "in Provence."

___

Quattro on Fourth   20 | 19 | 21 | $53
2611 W. 4th Ave. (Trafalgar St.), 604-734-4444;
www.quattrorestaurants.com
"On a wintry night" when only "solid" Italian dishes will do, West
Side diners warm to this "civilised" spot for "delicious" "handmade pastas" and other "satisfying" fare; the staff has "a lovely
way of treating people", and the space is "inviting", so if a few
find it "expensive", friends feel that "it's like visiting family –
without the dysfunction."

Raincity Grill   25 | 19 | 24 | $53
1193 Denman St. (Morton Ave.), 604-685-7337;
www.raincitygrill.com
"For a true taste of Vancouver", regionalists rave about this
"Pacific Northwest winner" with its "commitment to local suppli-
ers", "seasonal" "menu variations that keep it interesting" and an
"incredible" BC wine list; add "terrific" service and a "fabulous"
West End setting "with an English Bay view", and this spot "defines
West Coast" dining; N.B. a redo may outdate the Decor score.

Rare ◐ ⌧   – | – | – | E
1355 Hornby St. (bet. Drake & Pacific Sts.), 604-669-1256;
www.rarevancouver.com
True to its name, this Downtown newcomer emphasizes hard-to-
find ingredients, distinctive Pacific Northwest preparations and
a seasonally driven menu backed up by well-chosen local
wines; the sleek, compact duplex space is divided into a tasting
bar and dining lounge.

Rodney's Oyster House   23 | 17 | 18 | $40
1228 Hamilton St. (bet. Davie & Drake Sts.), 604-609-0080
"It's all about the oysters" at this "quality raw bar" serving "top-
notch" shellfish and other simple seafood, including "chowder
with attitude"; with its "raucous", "friendly vibe", it's a "great
place to hang out", so bivalve boosters put up with "spotty" service
for "one of the least pretentious meals you can have in Yaletown."

Salade de Fruits Café ⌧ ⇄   22 | 13 | 18 | $28
French Cultural Ctr., 1551 W. 7th Ave. (bet. Fir & Granville Sts.),
604-714-5987; www.saladedefruits.com
"Practise your French and enjoy *un bon repas*" of "great mussels
and pommes frites" or other bistro classics at this "cosy", "little"

"secret" inside the French Cultural Centre; even if "you need a shoehorn to get in" and the staff can be "cheeky", *amis* insist that this Francophilic "heaven" serves "unbeatable food for the price."

Salathai Thai   22 | 16 | 20 | $26

102-888 Burrard St. (bet. Robson & Smithe Sts.), 604-683-7999
3364 Cambie St. (bet. W. 17th & W. 18th Aves.), 604-875-6999;
www.salathai.ca

"Thai me up and feed me" declare devotees of this "dependable" West Side and Downtown duo that's "recommended for an authentic culinary experience"; adults dig the "value pricing" and service "with smiles", and "even picky kids" enjoy the "solid specialties", though heat-seekers wish they'd "crank it up spicewise."

Salmon House on the Hill   22 | 24 | 21 | $49

2229 Folkestone Way (Hwy. 1, 21st St. exit), West Vancouver,
604-926-3212; www.salmonhouse.com

"Every seat offers" a "stunning" "panorama" "of the city, mountains and water" at this West Van "favourite" that's "a hit with out-of-town guests" or "for family celebrations"; among the seafood-centric Pacific Northwest dishes, the alder-grilled "salmon is not to be missed" at this "very BC experience" that "blends native art and a creative menu."

Saltlik Steakhouse   ∇ 21 | 21 | 21 | $50

1032 Alberni St. (bet. Burrard & Thurlow Sts.), 604-689-9749;
www.saltlik.com

Early opinions are mixed on this steakhouse set in a glamorous Downtown space with a working fireplace; some are licking up the "good food", while others lash "it's a shame that this great room has been wasted" – if your meal "doesn't cut it", at least you can watch the "wannabe-actress servers" climb the ladder to "the unique raised wine cellar."

Saveur ⊠   – | – | – | E

850 Thurlow St. (Haro St.), 604-688-1633

"Don't judge the book by its cover" instruct enthusiasts of this quiet West End bistro "tucked away" off Robson that's run by "conscientious" chef Stephane Meyer and his wife, Nathalie; surveyors report "fantastic French" nouvelle fare and "friendly service", "as well as excellent tips on wine selections" to pair with the evolving prix fixe menu.

Savory Coast   ▽ 21 17 21 $54
1133 Robson St. (bet. Bute & Thurlow Sts.), 604-642-6278;
www.savorycoast.ca
Fans of chef Romy Prasad (ex Cin Cin) hike the stairs to this expansive "Romanesque room" in the West End for his "competent"
Mediterranean cuisine; in warm weather, diners nab perches on
the "fabulous" south-facing patio to be served by a "personable
but not intrusive" staff at this "new addition to the scene."

Sawasdee Thai   23 15 23 $30
4250 Main St. (bet. E. 26th & E. 27th Aves.), 604-876-4030;
www.sawasdeethairestaurant.com
"Everything is worth sampling" at this "long-time favourite" that
pleases patrons with its "mouth-watering", "home-style" Thai
fare; the "charming" staff "keeps you coming back" to the "delightful, little" East Side room, especially when you want to "spice
up your taste buds – and your life."

Seasons Hill Top Bistro   22 25 23 $55
Queen Elizabeth Park, Cambie St. (W. 33rd Ave.), 604-874-8008;
www.seasonshilltopbistro.com
"Take your rich maiden aunt" "to eat and dream" over "million-
dollar views" at this "tranquil" room "in a breathtaking setting
atop Queen Elizabeth Park"; the staff is "attentive", and the Pacific
Northwest plates are "of a high caliber", though some "would
like to see more imaginative dishes" at this "tourist magnet."

Senova   ▽ 19 21 19 $55
1864 W. 57th Ave. (East Blvd.), 604-266-8643
"Don't miss the Sunday paella" or "another one of their specialty
nights" at this "traditional yet creative" Portuguese newcomer to
a "quiet" West Side area; "likeable owner" Manuel Ferreira has
created a "relaxed" setting (as well as a "good wine list"), and
most praise the "powerful Iberian flavours lustily served up" from
the "open kitchen", even if some are "underwhelmed."

SEQUOIA GRILL AT THE TEAHOUSE   23 26 23 $52
(fka The Teahouse)
Stanley Park, 7501 Stanley Park Dr. (Ferguson Point), 604-669-3281;
www.vancouverdine.com
"Sit on the patio and watch the sun set" or "ask for a seat in the
conservatory (it's like dining in an English Garden)" at this "gor-

geous" West End spot "overlooking the water" with "the best views in Stanley Park"; though the "attentive" staff at this "enjoyable" Pacific Northwester delivers an "excellent brunch" and a "refined lunch", it's the scenery that's "king."

Shanghai Chinese Bistro   23 | 16 | 21 | $34

1124 Alberni St. (bet. Bute & Thurlow Sts.), 604-683-8222

"Don't miss" "the flamboyant noodle-making demonstration" advise enthusiasts of this second-floor Chinese restaurant Downtown where the "brisk, efficient" staff "takes great pride in their work and it shows"; the "classic" fare is "well prepared" with "fresh ingredients", though a few critics quibble that they've "had better."

Shao-Lin Noodle House   22 | 6 | 15 | $14

548 W. Broadway (bet. Ash & Cambie Sts.), 604-873-1816

"Follow the locals" – and "take the kids" – to this West Side storefront for "unbeatable handmade noodles right out of the cauldron" and other Northern Chinese dishes cooked for "an amazing price"; "watching the chefs create" "your meal right in front of you" ("and you thought your hair was difficult to manage?") is wonderful "entertainment" at this "complete dive" where the "slurping food" "is always great."

Shijo Japanese   23 | 17 | 19 | $42

202-1926 W. 4th Ave. (bet. Cypress & Maple Sts.), 604-732-4676; www.shijo.ca

Fin fans who head upstairs to this West Side room "check out the ever-changing specials board" for "delectable, fresh" sushi that "is a cut above" other joints'; regulars recommend the "great *toro*" and "particularly good sashimi" and note that "the guy on the robata grill is a master", even if the floor staff "can be slow" at this "traditional Japanese experience."

Shiro Japanese   23 | 9 | 18 | $26

3096 Cambie St. (W. 15th Ave.), 604-874-0027

"You can pay more, but sushi doesn't get much better than this" insist insiders who've "stepped into this authentic Japanese", a "long-renowned" West Sider in a strip mall near City Hall; whether you "want a home-cooked meal" or need your "raw fix taken care of", "forget the decor and the tiny space" 'cause fish any fresher would "swim to your table."

Shiru-Bay Chopstick Café ❶   25 | 20 | 18 | $38
1193 Hamilton St. (Davie St.), 604-408-9315; www.shiru-bay.com
With "tapas-style Japanese fusion" "all the rage", the "creative
small plates" – "oh, those *ebi chili mayo* prawns! – and "inventive drinks" "keep 'em lining up" at this "noisy" Yaletowner; even
if "service can be spotty", it's "fun with a group" coo customers
who crown it one of "the kings of Vancouver's *izakaya* world."

Simply Thai   23 | 16 | 19 | $30
1211 Hamilton St. (bet. Davie & Drake Sts.), 604-642-0123;
www.simplythairestaurant.com
Siamese savants savour "authentic dishes" like "fantastic" *cho
muang* purple dumplings at this "refined" Yaletown spot, whose
"staff visits Thailand for refresher courses"; while the service
can be "spicier than the food", chef-owner Grace Rerksuttisiridach
is "delightful" and "lunch is a great bargain."

Stella's Tap & Tapas Bar ❶   23 | 22 | 20 | $30
1191 Commercial Dr. (William St.), 604-254-2437; www.stellasbeer.com
A "breath of fresh air on the Drive", this "unique tapas bar" is a
"mecca for beer connoisseurs", "featuring a very good selection
of Belgian" suds along with "delicious, affordable" Asian fusion
small plates; even if "that pint takes awhile", it arrives "well
poured", so East Siders say this "casual player" "is just what
the neighbourhood needed."

Stepho's Souvlaki Greek Taverna ❶   20 | 13 | 18 | $21
1124 Davie St. (bet. Bute & Thurlow Sts.), 604-683-2555
"If you can stand the wait, it's worth it" assert Hellenic hopefuls
hankering for "comfort cuisine" served "in abundance" by a
"friendly staff" at this West End "institution"; "it's cheap and fill-
ing, but there's no need to stand in line for good Greek food
in Vancouver" shrug critics who "wonder" at queues for fare
that's "not exceptional."

Sun Sui Wah Seafood   24 | 16 | 17 | $34
3888 Main St. (E. 23rd Ave.), 604-872-8822
Alderbridge Pl., 4940 No. 3 Rd. (bet. Alderbridge Way & Alexandra Rd.),
Richmond, 604-273-8208
"Grab what you can from the passing carts" but "don't neglect
the menu" suggest admirers of the "world-class dim sum" at this
"crowded" Chinese duo on the East Side and in Richmond; "sea-

food has never tasted so fresh", so despite "uneven service", "bring 12 of your best friends and enjoy a banquet."

Szechuan Chongqing
22 | 10 | 16 | $25

2808 Commercial Dr. (E. 12th Ave.), 604-254-7434
"Order something with chili and garlic" (and "don't miss the green beans") at this East Sider where the "spicy" fare is "consistently good"; though the interior "leaves something to be desired" and the service earns mixed reviews, adherents "would not hesitate to recommend it to anyone looking for excellent Szechuan."

Takis Taverna
∇ 22 | 15 | 19 | $25

1106 Davie St. (bet. Bute & Thurlow Sts.), 604-682-1336
Regulars "don't want to reveal" that (even when the queue at "Stepho's is unbearable") there are "no lineups" at this "intimate" West Ender for "excellent" Greek food "at very reasonable prices"; the fare is "authentic", the staff is "friendly" and sweet-tooths say the crème caramel is "one of the best we've ever tasted."

Tapastree
23 | 18 | 22 | $39

1829 Robson St. (bet. Denman & Gilford Sts.), 604-606-4680; www.tapastree.ca
The "finely executed", "innovative" Pacific Northwest tapas at this "well-kept West End secret" are "so good" they "should be illegal"; "don't come if you don't like sharing", but if you do, the "fantastic service", "fun atmosphere" and "yummy" small plates might seem like "the best idea in dining out since God invented food."

TOJO'S ☒
27 | 16 | 23 | $73

202-777 W. Broadway (bet. Heather & Willow Sts.), 604-872-8050; www.tojos.com
For some of "the best sushi in North America", "put yourself in the hands" of chef-owner Tojo Hidekazu and order the "mind-blowing omakase", then "taste pure decadence" in an array of "inventive" "nouvelle" creations; "overlook the Howard Johnson decor" in this "undisputed winner" on the West Side and "experience Japanese food heaven – in credit-card-limit hell."

Tomahawk Barbecue
19 | 16 | 18 | $18

1550 Philip Ave. (off Marine Dr.), North Vancouver, 604-988-2612; www.tomahawkrestaurant.com
"Its mixed grill might make your cardiologist do back flips", but breakfast at this "family-owned" diner adorned "with First

Nations artifacts" is "a must"; this "North Shore institution" has served "good, basic chow" and "lots of it", with "super-friendly service" and "kitschy" "charm" since 1926; heck, the Yukon bacon alone is "worth the trip."

Tomato Fresh Food Cafe   20 | 16 | 17 | $27
3305 Cambie St. (W. 17th Ave.), 604-874-6020;
www.tomatofreshfoodcafe.com
For "comfort food" with "no surprises", West Siders head to this "laid-back" Pacific Northwester that serves "tasty", "healthy" fare for three meals square at "a great bargain"; the staff is "friendly" – if "slow" – in this "funky", "relaxed" "neighbourhood favourite."

Topanga Cafe ⑤   20 | 14 | 17 | $22
2904 W. 4th Ave. (bet. Bayswater & MacDonald Sts.), 604-733-3713;
www.topangacafe.com
"When you can't drive to Bellingham", the Cal-Mex staples are "more than acceptable" at this "tiny" West Side "hangout" where "nothing has changed for years"; there's "usually a wait" to sit, but you can pass time perusing the "walls adorned" with place mats "coloured by patrons using restaurant-supplied crayons."

Toshi   ▽ 26 | 16 | 19 | $24
181 E. 16th Ave. (bet. Main & Quebec Sts.), 604-874-5173
The "fabulous" sushi and other "authentic" Japanese fare is "a hit" at this "tiny gem" on the East Side; with "immaculate" premises, "prompt service" and "amazingly inexpensive prices", no wonder pleased patrons put up with "lineups" – some even "travel across the city for their fix."

Trafalgar's Bistro   23 | 16 | 22 | $39
2603 W. 16th Ave. (Trafalgar St.), 604-739-0555;
www.trafalgars.com
"Unexpectedly cutting-edge" Eclectic dishes that "change with the seasons", paired with a "great wine selection", draw devotees to this "unassuming" West Side bistro; while cheapskates charge that it's "expensive", everyone agrees that it's worth "saving room" for the "out-of-this-world" desserts – there are usually at least 30 of them.

Tropika Malaysian Cuisine   20 | 15 | 16 | $27
2975 Cambie St. (W. 14th Ave.), 604-879-6002
1128 Robson St. (bet. Bute & Thurlow Sts.), 604-737-6002

(continued)
Tropika Malaysian Cuisine
Aberdeen Centre, 4151 Hazelbridge Way (Cambie Rd.), Richmond, 604-233-7002
www.tropika-canada.com
The Malaysian, Singaporean and Thai dishes are "great for sharing" at this "reliable", "inexpensive" trio that "hits the spot" for locals and "homesick expats"; still, critics complain about "spotty service", flavours "adapted to Western tastes" and portions "too small" "to fill an average hungry person."

Vera's Burger Shack   23 | 8 | 13 | $13 |
1935 Cornwall Ave. (bet. Cypress & Walnut Sts.), 604-228-8372
1030 Davie St. (bet. Burrard & Thurlow Sts.), 604-893-8372
1181 Denman St. (bet. Morton Ave. & Pendrell St.), 604-681-5450
2188 Western Pkwy. (Dalhousie Rd.), 604-221-8372
Dundarave Pier (Bellevue Ave.), West Vancouver, 604-603-8372
www.verasburgershack.com
"You can't beat Vera's meat!" chorus carnivores chomping through "thick, juicy", "monster"-sized patties of "artery-clogging potential" that "help to keep local cardiologists in business"; "awesome" tempura-battered onion rings and orders of fries that "feed at least two" make up for "limited seating" and "no service to speak of" at this quintet of "havens, if it's a burger you're cravin'."

VIJ'S   28 | 22 | 25 | $46 |
1480 W. 11th Ave. (bet. Granville & Hemlock Sts.), 604-736-6664;
www.vijs.ca
"Every meal is a sensual experience" at "consummate host" Vikram Vij's West Sider, known equally for the "genial" chef-owner's "personal touches" and for the "world-class", "inventive interpretations" of Indian cuisine; while "the single detractor is a no-reservations policy" that can lead to "hour-plus lineups", the "back lounge is the best cocktail party in town" with "complimentary tasty treats" to "soothe the wait."

Vij's Rangoli   26 | 19 | 20 | $22 |
1488 W. 11th Ave. (bet. Granville & Hemlock Sts.), 604-736-5711;
www.vijs.ca
"If you don't want to face the wait next door", or if you're looking for the "best bet for lunch" on the West Side, this "poor-man's Vij's" is "a cheaper, quicker alternative", offering a "limited se-

lection" of "succulent" Indian fusion dishes; with the option to
bring these "big flavours" home in the frozen "take-out boil-in
bags", the "time-stressed" wonder "who cooks anymore."

Villa del Lupo   26 | 23 | 26 | $60
869 Hamilton St. (bet. Robson & Smithe Sts.), 604-688-7436;
www.villadellupo.com
"Take a date" (or "your trophy wife") "for a romantic rendezvous"
at this "intimate", "elegant" Downtown heritage house where the
"superb service" "makes you feel like royalty", and the "high-
end" Italian–Pacific Northwest fare is "outstanding"; the "artfully
presented plates" are matched with an "excellent wine list" for a
meal that is "*delicioso* in any language."

WATERMARK ON KITS BEACH   17 | 27 | 17 | $43
1305 Arbutus St. (Creelman Ave.), 604-738-5487;
www.watermarkrestaurant.ca
The "amazing water views" complement the *Vancouver Survey's*
No.1 for Decor at this "modernist cube" that may have "the best
location in town" directly on the West Side's Kitsilano Beach; the
Pacific Northwest fare is "ho-hum", and the service "hit-or-miss",
but stop by for "drinks and appetizers" "on a summer night" when
the "impressive" "sunsets can make you forget about the food."

Water St. Café   20 | 18 | 20 | $34
300 Water St. (Cambie St.), 604-689-2832
"Tourists and business lunchers" dine on Pacific Northwest–
Italian fare served by an "amiable staff" at this "long-time
favourite" set in an "attractive heritage room with exposed
brick" across the street from Gastown's "famous steam clock";
through the "magnificent windows", you can watch "people
walking by", which may help to distract you from what some say
is an "unexceptional" meal.

WEST   29 | 26 | 27 | $79
2881 Granville St. (W. 13th Ave.), 604-738-8938; www.westrestaurant.com
Ranked No. 1 for Food in the *Vancouver Survey*, this "jewel in the
city's culinary crown" is "exquisite in every way"; chef David
Hawksworth creates "extraordinary" Pacific Northwest "dishes
with divine flavours" that are paired with "superb" wines "gra-
ciously served" by an "exemplary" staff in a "stunning" West
Side room; "it'll cost you a pretty penny", but for a "superlative"

experience that will have "you floating home in a state of perfect serenity", "go West as quickly as possible."

Wild Garlic   20 | 17 | 21 | $35
2120 W. Broadway (bet. Arbutus & Yew Sts.), 604-730-0880
Wild Garlic Bistro
792 Denman St. (bet. Alberni & Robson Sts.), 604-687-1663
www.wildgarlic.com
"If you love garlic" (especially slow-roasted), these "warm" West Side and West End siblings are "the places to go"; while not every Pacific Northwest dish on the "innovative" menu features the stinking rose, most of them do, in "both subtle and overwhelming" amounts, so bulb-lovers insist that they're "worth checking out."

Wild Rice ❶   21 | 23 | 18 | $36
117 W. Pender St. (bet. Abbott & Cambie Sts.), 604-642-2882;
www.wildricevancouver.com
There are "no sweet-and-sour chicken balls" at this "trendy" Downtowner that "fuses traditional Chinese and modern West Coast" flavours into "funkier-than-funky" share plates; "wear black" and mingle with the "young and beautiful" over "imaginative cocktails" in a "chic", "minimalist" room, where "hot servers" and a "cool vibe" make up for the "inconsistent eats."

William Tell Restaurant, The   24 | 21 | 25 | $60
Georgian Court Hotel, 765 Beatty St. (bet. Robson & W. Georgia Sts.),
604-688-3504; www.thewmtell.com
You "can't go wrong with the tried and true" say loyalists who "love the old-world charm" of this "intimate" Downtowner that's served "top-notch" Swiss fare since 1964; though the space may "need a serious update", the service is still "superb", and the "Sunday evening Farmer's Buffet" "is really something to yodel about."

VICTORIA & VANCOUVER ISLAND

Aerie Resort Dining Room, The   26 | 25 | 26 | $79
The Aerie Resort, 600 Ebedora Ln. (Spectacle Lake turnoff),
Malahat, 250-743-7115; www.aerie.bc.ca
Culinary climbers ascend to this "mountaintop paradise" for the height of "decadence"; the French-influenced Pacific Northwest cuisine is "gastronomically out of this world", and the multi-

course tastings paired with "a stunning wine list" are "works of art"; the staff is "amazing", while the "spectacular views" are "for the gods", making this "special-occasion" splurge "worth the trip" up the Malahat.

Arbutus Grille & Wine Bar   25 | 25 | 23 | $64
Brentwood Bay Lodge & Spa, 849 Verdier Ave. (W. Saanich Rd.),
Brentwood Bay, 250-544-2079; www.brentwoodbaylodge.com
The "elegant" Brentwood Bay Lodge's glass-and-cedar-trimmed dining room delivers Pacific Northwest fare that's "as good" as the "fabulous" views; the menu is filled with "fantastic finds" like the Harvest of the Sea, served in a handcrafted Haida-inspired dish, and the staff "points you toward the best" wines on the "outstanding" list; N.B. a recent chef change may outdate the Food score.

Blue Crab Bar & Grill, The   24 | 24 | 22 | $49
Coast Victoria Harbourside Hotel & Marina, 146 Kingston St.
(Montreal St., waterfront), Victoria, 250-480-1999;
www.bluecrab.ca
"Breathtaking" views of "Victoria's busy harbour" dotted with "floatplanes, sailboats and kayakers" draw seafood seekers to this "dependable" Downtowner for "superior" fin fare and "good BC wines"; fans "never tire" of the "picturesque" vistas and "friendly, personal service."

Blue Fox Cafe, The   21 | 16 | 22 | $18
101-919 Fort St. (Quadra St.), Victoria, 250-380-1683
"Hearty", "good-value" options "start your morning" right at this "bright", "little" Downtown Eclectic where lunch is "amazing" too; "huge portions" that "challenge the biggest appetites" create weekend lineups "down the street", but the foxy insist that the "joie de vivre atmosphere" makes it "worth the wait."

Brasserie L'Ecole ⊠   26 | 22 | 24 | $46
1715 Government St. (Pandora Ave.), Victoria, 250-475-6260;
www.lecole.ca
Ruling a "gastronomic heaven" that takes "a slow approach to the pleasures of the table", chef-owner Sean Brennan is "king in his kitchen" at this "superb" French bistro Downtown; the "cosy space" and the menu may be "small, but the flavours are large", created from "locally sourced ingredients" and paired with "a

wide choice of wine by the glass" (and around 40 Belgian beers); service is "impeccable" too.

Cafe Brio
25 | 23 | 23 | $48

944 Fort St. (bet. Quadra & Vancouver Sts.), Victoria, 250-383-0009; www.cafe-brio.com

Chef Chris Dignan's "creative", "seasonal" Pacific Northwest cuisine, combined with one of "the most accessible wine lists in town", hits high notes at this Downtowner with a "lively Tuscan" feel; plus, the "friendly" owners "take care of you like you were a beloved member of their family."

CAMILLE'S
27 | 22 | 26 | $53

45 Bastion Sq. (bet. Fort & Yates Sts.), Victoria, 250-381-3433; www.camillesrestaurant.com

"The place to go for that special occasion", this "Victoria institution" located in a 1900 heritage building Downtown serves "sumptuous, exquisitely created" Pacific Northwest dishes matched with wines from a "superb" list; the service is "subtle" and "attentive", and despite doubters who declare the "dark" ambiance "more dungeon than candlelit romantic", the overall experience is "outstanding."

Deep Cove Chalet
25 | 25 | 26 | $57

11190 Chalet Rd. (Tatlow Rd.), Sidney, 250-656-3541; www.deepcovechalet.com

"There aren't enough superlatives" to describe this Sidney waterside destination that lures "even discerning connoisseurs"; in "one of the most enchanting locations on the planet", the "enormous" wine cellar offers "an extraordinary abundance of choices" (nearly 18,000 bottles), and the "splendidly prepared classical French" fare, with a few twists from "eccentric" chef-owner Pierre Koffel, is "superb."

Dock 503
23 | 22 | 24 | $49

Van Isle Marina, 2320 Harbour Rd. (bet. Bowden & Griffiths Rds.), Sidney, 250-656-0828; dock503.vanislemarina.com

"True foodies" dock at this "stylish" Pacific Northwest restaurant "in the heart of Van Isle Marina" in Sidney near the Swartz Bay ferry; a "trendy", seasonally focused menu "concentrating on local ingredients" offers "many choices", all "beautifully served" at this "treasured secret."

Empress Room   25 | 28 | 26 | $55

The Fairmont Empress, 721 Government St. (bet. Belleville &
Humboldt Sts.), Victoria, 250-389-2727; www.fairmont.com
"When you want to get pampered", the "sublime" Pacific
Northwest food, "seamless black-tie service" and "exquisite",
"plush" setting in the venerable Empress hotel Downtown
combine for a "once-in-a-lifetime experience" that'll "make
you feel damned special"; "enjoy a martini in the Bengal Lounge"
before a meal that might be "priced for kings" but is "well
worth the indulgence."

Ferris' Oyster Bar & Grill   23 | 18 | 20 | $26

536 Yates St. (bet. Government & Wharf Sts.), Victoria,
250-360-1824
"Expect a lineup" at this "classic", "casual" seafooder
Downtown where "locals and tourists alike" "rub shoulders"
for "barrels of oysters" and "terrific yam fries"; the staff is "fun",
and the "atmosphere is comfortable", so if some shuckers shun
the "funky", "often chaotic" room with its "chairs packed
so tightly", others happily shell out a few clams for chow that's
"reliable" and "fresh."

HASTINGS HOUSE   27 | 26 | 28 | $74

Hastings House Country Inn, 160 Upper Ganges Rd.
(Fulford Ganges Rd.), Salt Spring Island, 250-537-2362;
www.hastingshouse.com
"Pamper me and never make me leave" beg visitors to this
"classy country-house" "king of the islands", rated No. 1 for Food
and Service in and around Vancouver Island; not only is the
Pacific Northwest fare "terrific" ("fantastic Salt Spring lamb"),
but the whole experience is "perfection" for "when only the best
will do"; N.B. open mid-March to mid-November.

Il Terrazzo   24 | 24 | 22 | $44

555 Johnson St. (bet. Government & Wharf Sts.), Victoria,
250-361-0028; www.ilterrazzo.com
Amici "haven't met a meal they didn't love" at this "packed"
Northern Italian, "tucked away in a historic alley" Downtown,
where the staff makes you "feel welcome" with "huge plates of
pasta" and a "ridiculously large wine list"; it's "perfect for a romantic evening" "on the terrace by the fireplace", but even for
seating in the "boisterous" interior, reviewers "recommend it."

J & J Wonton Noodle House ⊠ 25 | 11 | 19 | $21

1012 Fort St. (bet. Cook & Vancouver Sts.), Victoria,
250-383-0680

Despite "the Formica", "fluorescent lights" and inevitable "line-ups", diehards "beat a trail to the door" of this "economical", "vegetarian-friendly" "Downtown noodle house" for some of the "best Chinese in town"; "so what if you feel rushed" in a "hole-in-the-wall" setting? – it's "well worth the pain" for "excellent" chow; N.B. lunch-only at press time.

KEG STEAKHOUSE & BAR, THE 20 | 18 | 20 | $38

500 Fort St. (Wharf St.), Victoria, 250-386-7789
3940 Quadra St. (bet. MacKenzie Ave. & Tattersal Dr.), Victoria,
250-479-1651
www.kegsteakhouse.com
See review in Vancouver section.

Marina Restaurant 21 | 24 | 23 | $43

1327 Beach Dr. (bet. Currie & Windsor Rds.), Victoria,
250-598-8555

"Location, location, location" lures old salts to this "gorgeous" room in Oak Bay, with "unbeatable" views of "yachts sailing by"; fresh fish tops the "safe", "solid" Pacific Northwest menu, and Sunday brunch – a "favourite local tradition" – remains "the buffet of the gods", even if some young-at-hearts consider "the atmosphere a little middle-aged."

Pagliacci's 21 | 19 | 21 | $27

1011 Broad St. (bet. Broughton & Fort Sts.), Victoria, 250-386-1662
"Strangers sit elbow to elbow" in this "narrow" Downtowner that's "abuzz with laughter and conversation", but it's worth the "squish" and "hustle-bustle" for "huge portions" of "moderately priced", "classic" Italian fare "served with a smile"; despite detractors who dub it "average", this long-time "staple" (with jazz several nights) remains among "the coolest hot spots in town."

Paprika Bistro 27 | 20 | 25 | $50

2524 Estevan Ave. (bet. Dunlevy Rd. & Musgrave St.), Victoria,
250-592-7424; www.paprika-bistro.com
Adventurers venture "off the beaten track" to this "small bistro" in Oak Bay to be "blown away" by the "tempting array" of "gourmet" dishes (like roast duck with sour cherry sauce) from chef

George Szasz's "innovative" French-Hungarian menu; insistence on "local" ingredients, an "amazing wine list" and "incredible service" add up to "a fantastic find" that's "miles above the rest."

Pescatore's Seafood & Grill ❂   23 | 21 | 21 | $42

614 Humboldt St. (bet. Gordon & Government Sts.), Victoria, 250-385-4512; www.pescatores.com

Cedar-planked salmon and more "hedonistic" choices ("crispy this and crab on that") pair with "fab martinis" and a "solid wine list" at this "unassuming" Pacific Northwest seafooder near the harbour Downtown; service is "spot-on", and lunchtime brings "affordable blue-plate specials", so no wonder it's "crowded" (and "noisy").

Pointe Restaurant at   24 | 28 | 23 | $75
Wickaninnish Inn, The

500 Osprey Ln. (Chesterman Beach, waterfront), Tofino, 250-725-3106; www.wickinn.com

When "there's a winter storm raging outside the huge panoramic windows", there are "not enough superlatives" to describe the "breathtaking" vistas from this "romantic" room (No. 1 for Decor on Vancouver Island) on "an amazing expanse of sandy beach" "at the end of the world" in Tofino; most enjoy the "inventive" Pacific Northwest cuisine and "wonderful" service, but even those who find the vibe "pretentious" agree that "the place is gorgeous."

Rebar Modern Food   24 | 20 | 18 | $25

50 Bastion Sq. (Langley St.), Victoria, 250-361-9223; www.rebarmodernfood.com

"Yes, soy beans can be gourmet" insist herbivores who hail the "vibrant food" at this Eclectic "veggie nirvana" (with some seafood), one of the "best organic hippie restaurants around"; the almond burger is even "better than the real thing", and while the "funky", "lime-green" "decor borders on the strange", a meal at this "groovy" Downtowner "leaves you feeling better than at the spa."

Restaurant Matisse   26 | 23 | 25 | $56

512 Yates St. (Wharf St.), Victoria, 250-480-0883; www.restaurantmatisse.com

The "elegant" classic French fare is "matched only by the attention you receive from gracious owner" John Phillips at this "darling, little spot" Downtown; advocates give broad-brush approval to the "always-changing menu" and the "outstanding wines" brought by "an amusing, knowledgeable staff", concluding it's *"magnifique."*

Rosemeade Dining Room, The   27 | 27 | 26 | $62

English Inn & Resort, 429 Lampson St. (Esquimalt Rd.), Victoria, 250-412-7673; www.englishinnresort.com

A "brilliant interior design" "with a strong culinary experience to back it up" is turning heads in Esquimalt, where the dining room at the English Inn & Resort has been redone with a "cool Euro look" and a "beautiful fireplace"; from the "excellent" Pacific Northwest fare to the "helpful staff", it's some of "the best fine dining Victoria offers."

Siam Thai   24 | 15 | 20 | $28

512 Fort St. (Langley St.), Victoria, 250-383-9911; www.siamthai.ca

"The food is so good, we always over-order" reveal regulars at this Downtown Siamese offering "nicely prepared" fare; while they often opt "for takeout" – "it can be hectic inside" – diners "keep going back" for "marvelous soups" and other "delicious" dishes.

Sobo   ∇ 26 | 15 | 20 | $22

1028 Pacific Rim Hwy. (Fellowship Dr.), Tofino, 250-725-2341

Tofino's "SOphisticated BOhemian delivers what's promised": "great organic food" that "sends your taste buds into a spin of delight"; locals "love the fish tacos", originally dished out from a "funky purple van" "in a parking lot" – they're still on the menu, with other Eclectic fare made from island-sourced ingredients in newer sit-down digs in the Botanical Gardens.

Sooke Harbour House   26 | 25 | 26 | $81

1528 Whiffen Spit Rd. (Hwy. 14), Sooke, 250-642-3421; www.sookeharbourhouse.com

"Local ingredients" with "a capital L" ("the chef harvests seaweed for dinner", "picks herbs" "in the kitchen gardens" and cooks "seafood caught that day") lure diners to this Pacific Northwest "trendsetter", known for its "intricate", "imaginative recipes" and a wine list so large it could be "a doorstop"; a "polished" staff manages the "charming" Sooke waterfront room, and while it's "expensive", "the flavours will rock your world."

Temple ◐   24 | 25 | 20 | $43
525 Fort St. (Langley St.), Victoria, 250-383-2313; www.thetemple.ca
"Hipsters" worship this modern space with a "big-city feel" inside
an 1890s building Downtown; though nonbelievers are skeptical
about "sketchy service" and culinary "inconsistency", adherents
praise the "adventurous" Pacific Northwest menu and note that
it's a rare "late-night option in a city that goes to bed at 10 PM."

Zambri's 🖾   27 | 15 | 23 | $37
*Harris Green Ctr., 110-911 Yates St. (bet. Quadra & Vancouver Sts.),
Victoria, 250-360-1171*
"Don't be fooled by the shopping-centre location" – chef/co-
owner Peter Zambri cooks the "best Italian food in the city" insist
amici of this "unpretentious" Downtown trattoria run by a "hos-
pitable" team; based on "simple, local" ingredients, the "flavourful" fare "never fails to excite the palate", and it's "a bargain."

WHISTLER

Après Restaurant & Wine Bar   20 | 23 | 22 | $61
*103-4338 Main St. (Northlands Blvd.), 604-935-0200;
www.apresrestaurant.com*
Diners duck into this "quiet, intimate" Modern European escape
in Whistler Village where the striking geometric decor and
"friendly" staff contribute to a "great atmosphere"; a "fine selection" of Northwest wines by the glass and the "outstanding" foie
gras platter have alpine eaters saying "who cares about skiing?"

Araxi Restaurant & Lounge   25 | 23 | 23 | $62
4222 Village Sq. (Whistler Way), 604-932-4540; www.araxi.com
The "well-heeled crowd" claims that this "classic" is "one of the
best" in the Village, thanks to the "Canadian-chic" setting,
"delicious" Pacific Northwest menu and "diverse" BC-based wine
list; "après-ski" fans of the "awesome raw bar" and "informative
staff" say after "more than two decades, this place still glows."

Aubergine Grille   21 | 18 | 21 | $48
*Westin Resort & Spa, 4090 Whistler Way (base of Whistler Mtn.),
604-935-4344; www.westin.com*
"Fresh local ingredients jazz up an array of wild game and seafood" at this Pacific Northwester in the Westin; enthusiasts "en-

joy the ambiance" stoked by an "open kitchen", but protesters who pout that the "large space feels cold" find it "uninspiring."

Bear Foot Bistro   23 | 20 | 22 | $85
Listel Whistler Hotel, 4121 Village Green (Whistler Way), 604-932-3433
Oenophiles envy a "wine list the size of *War and Peace*" at this "cosy" yet "elegant" Pacific Northwester, where the 1,600+ bottles pair with an "awesome" prix fixe menu including "game galore"; the "attentive" crew at this Village fixture "knows how to titillate the palate", and though "prices are not for the faint of heart", you can sup "in the bar for lots less."

Caramba! Restaurante   20 | 16 | 21 | $34
12-4314 Main St. (Town Plaza), 604-938-1879;
www.caramba-restaurante.com
After the slopes, hordes head to "one of Whistler's most popular spots" for "casual" Med fare, including "calamari to die for" and "good pizza and pasta" from the "wood-fired oven"; those with tots tout this Town Square spot's "family-oriented" feel and "friendly staff", while wallet-watchers warm to its "great price points."

Edgewater Lodge   ▽ 23 | 25 | 25 | $47
Green Lake, 8030 Alpine Way (Hwy. 99), 604-932-0688;
www.edgewater-lodge.com
For "unbeatable views", head to this Green Lake spot to savour "outstanding game dishes" from chef Thomas Piekarski's Pacific Northwest–Continental menu; a "nice, quiet place for dinner", it may be "out of the way", but diners declare it "worth the cab fare."

FIFTY TWO 80 BISTRO   27 | 27 | 27 | $62
Four Seasons Resort Whistler, 4591 Blackcomb Way (Lorimer Rd.),
604-935-3400; www.fourseasons.com
"Elegance is in vogue" at this "resort jewel" in the Upper Village that is tops in Whistler for Food, Decor and Service with "first-class, sophisticated" Pacific Northwest fare, a "typically superior Four Seasons" staff and a "slick", "contemporary" look; sure, it's "pricey", but it merits "a special trip – from anywhere."

Hy's Steakhouse   22 | 21 | 23 | $60
Delta Whistler Village Suites, 4308 Main St. (Northlands Blvd.),
604-905-5555
"Hungry carnivores" claim you "can never go wrong" with the "perfectly prepared", hearty portions of meat served "with great

spirit" in a "typical steakhouse setting" at this "Whistler favourite"; however, those who find this sib to Vancouver's Hy's Encore "expensive", say "it's hyped up way more than it should be."

Il Caminetto di Umberto
25 | 21 | 23 | $55

4242 Village Stroll (Whistler Village Sq.), 604-932-4442

You "feel like you're in Italy" at this "touch of Tuscany" "in the heart of Whistler" serving "authentic" Italian in an "elegant yet comfortable" room; with owner Umberto Menghi's "exceptional staff" to "make sure everything is the best", it's an "après-ski highlight", though "it can be challenging to get a table on busy weekends."

KEG STEAKHOUSE & BAR, THE
20 | 18 | 20 | $38

Whistler Village Inn, 4429 Sundial Pl. (Whistler Village Sq.), 604-932-5151; www.kegsteakhouse.com

See review in Vancouver section.

La Rua Restaurante
25 | 23 | 24 | $60

Le Chamois, 4557 Blackcomb Way (bet. Glacier Dr. & Lorimer Rd.), 604-932-5011; www.larua-restaurante.com

Slopesters seeking a "nice space for après ski" slide into these "wonderful" Med-style rooms in Le Chamois hotel, where the "rich" Pacific Northwest cuisine is "done right"; "friendly proprietor" Mario Enero sees to it that "you're not disappointed" with a meal that can include signature reindeer medallions.

Monk's Grill
20 | 18 | 20 | $42

4555 Blackcomb Way (Lorimer Rd.), 604-932-9677

Diners "can't get much closer to the hill" than this "laid-back" Eclectic "at the bottom of Blackcomb" Mountain; it's a "perfect place for a drink" or for "a relaxing night out", though some say the food, which ranges from steak and seafood in the dining room to burgers and wings in the lounge, is just "average."

Quattro at Whistler
23 | 23 | 22 | $66

Pinnacle International Hotel, 4319 Main St. (Northlands Blvd.), 604-905-4844; www.quattrorestaurants.com

"This place does good Italian", say *amici* of this Pinnacle International Hotel mainstay, where the antipasto misto and "great pasta" come out of an "accommodating kitchen"; the "classy", high-ceilinged room features "dark woods" and two fireplaces, and the staff "ensures you enjoy yourself."

RIM ROCK CAFE
26 | 23 | 24 | $59

2117 Whistler Rd. (Hwy. 99), 604-932-5565; www.rimrockwhistler.com
The "unsurpassed" Pacific Northwest "seafood and wild game specialties" (including "superb caribou") "never fail to impress" schussers at this "cosy room" in Whistler; it's a "romantic", "relaxing sojourn from the busy scene", with "great service" "for a post-ski feast", even if wallet-watchers warn "get someone else to pay."

Splitz Grill
24 | 12 | 16 | $14

104-4369 Main St. (Northlands Blvd.), 604-938-9300
"Choose from a mountain of toppings to make a mountain of a burger" at this "perfect spot" "for a cheap eat out" in Whistler; the patties are "the best ever", and the "awesome onion rings" and poutine (fries with cheese curds and gravy) are "almost worth the eventual bypass."

Sushi Village
23 | 16 | 20 | $35

4272 Mountain Sq. (Whistler Village Sq.), 604-932-3330; www.sushivillage.com
"Young skiers and hot snowbunnies" make this "packed" Whistler Village Japanese the "place to hang" "right where you need it, at the mountain's base" – particularly if what you need is to eat "benchmark" sushi, "made by a friendly chef who caters" "to your needs"; "be prepared to wait" because the "innovative rolls" are "worth it."

Sushi Ya
20 | 13 | 20 | $35

230-4370 Lorimer Rd. (Whistler Village N.), 604-905-0155
"Go early to avoid the lineup" for "wonderful tempura" and raw "fish so fresh you'll think it was still breathing" at this "simple" Japanese upstairs at the Village North Marketplace; it's "great for takeout or a quick eat-in", even if spoilers suggest "the name should be 'Sushi No.'"

Trattoria di Umberto
26 | 22 | 23 | $57

Mountainside Lodge, 4417 Sundial Pl. (Whistler Village Sq.), 604-932-5858; www.umbertos.com
"Culinary genius" Umberto Menghi's Village Square trattoria is a "perennial favourite" for "authentic" Italian fare served in an "elegant but casual atmosphere"; "great service" and bar seating overlooking "the kitchen staff doing its thing" make it "fabulous"

for dinner, but "the real secret is to ski down for lunch" to enjoy "a gourmet feast" for little more than "the price of a crappy burger on the slopes."

Val d'Isère Brasserie
23 | 21 | 22 | $49

8-4314 Main St. (Town Plaza), 604-932-4666
Though it's "hard to beat" chef-owner Roland Pfaff's veal with morels, aficionados advise "you'll be glad you explored something new" too, at this "attractive" "European brasserie" in the Town Plaza; the "imaginative" French fare is "well prepared", the 300-bottle wine list includes "lovely" selections and the service is "fine", so "you will not be disappointed."

Wildflower, The
23 | 22 | 22 | $55

Chateau Whistler Resort, 4599 Chateau Blvd. (Blackcomb Way), 604-938-2033; www.fairmont.com
Loyalists "love the view", matched by "super service" in the "Fairmont style, where they wait on you hand and foot", at this dining room in the Chateau Whistler Resort; the "varied" Pacific Northwest "menu showcases BC ingredients", and the setting feels "first-class"; P.S. "Sunday brunch is great here too."

Nightlife

VANCOUVER

Most Popular	Top Appeal
1. Opus Bar	*26* Commodore Ballrm.
2. Commodore Ballrm.	Bacchus Lounge
3. Bacchus Lounge	*24* Railway Club
4. Celebrities	*23* Opus Bar
5. Shark Club	*21* Ginger Sixty Two

	A	D	S	$
AuBar Nightclub	18	18	19	$9

674 Seymour St. (bet. Dunsmuir & Georgia Sts.), 604-648-2228; www.aubarnightclub.com

"Beautiful people" head to this "trendy" club Downtown to dance to DJ-spun hip-hop, R&B and reggae; a "friendly staff" caters to "upbeat" "professionals" who "love the nightlife", even if a few barflies flit past, complaining "there's always a wait" to party among the "pretentious."

BACCHUS LOUNGE | 26 | 26 | 23 | $12 |

Wedgewood Hotel, 845 Hornby St. (bet. Robson & Smithe Sts.), 604-689-7777; www.wedgewoodhotel.com

"As many wedding rings slip on as off" at this "plush" lounge in the Wedgewood Hotel that admirers agree is the "classiest joint in town"; everyone from "Downtown business types" to "tony" "thirty- and fortysomethings" appreciates the "fantastic martinis" made by the "excellent" "old-school bartenders", "even if the tabs make you wish you were on an expense account."

Bar None | 21 | 17 | 16 | $9 |

1222 Hamilton St. (bet. Davie & Drake Sts.), 604-689-7000; www.barnonenightclub.com

For "down-to-earth" dancing to "great live" R&B and soul, head to this "homey" club in a converted Yaletown warehouse on weeknights when house band Soulstream makes waves; though other acts can be "hit-or-miss", the "diverse, sexy" (if "slightly older") crowd is "fun" and "friendly."

Celebrities | 21 | 21 | 19 | $11 |

1022 Davie St. (bet. Burrard & Thurlow Sts.), 604-681-6180; www.celebritiesnightclub.com

"Where gay guys go to party and straight girls go to dance", this "fantastic" "mixed club" on the West End draws "all kinds of people"; regulars recommend the "upper viewing level" at this "Vancouver legend" where you can look down on a crowd grooving "on the wild side (or at least a little more open mindedly)" to "music that kicks."

Cellar Nightclub | 18 | 18 | 19 | $10 |

1006 Granville St. (Nelson St.), 604-605-4350; www.cellarvan.com

With "great" rock bands and "bartenders that you want to take home", this "high-end" Downtown club below Doolin's Irish Pub attracts a "hot", "younger crowd"; you "do feel like you're in a cellar", albeit a "stylish, urban" one with cobblestone floors, stone archways and wood-beamed ceilings – just beware, because the joint is also "a true meat market."

COMMODORE BALLROOM, THE   26 | 24 | 21 | $10
868 Granville St. (bet. Robson & Smithe Sts.), 604-739-4550;
www.hob.com
"My dad used to swing here during World War II" say fans of this
1929 Downtown "institution", "the best live venue" for "any big
event"; "get your dancing shoes on" because the "sprung floor"
makes "jumping up and down" "so much fun", and with a
"friendly staff", "it's no mystery why" it's "been popular for so long."

Crush Champagne Lounge   20 | 19 | 17 | $10
Howard Johnson, 1180 Granville St. (Davie St.), 604-684-0355;
www.crushlounge.ca
"A nice place for the not-20-anymore crowd" who "love those
couches", this Downtown lounge lives up to its name with many
bubblies to sip to a soundtrack of jazz, R&B and soul; still, snobs
slam it as "so-so", with "trainwreck DJs" spinning "schmaltz."

Ginger Sixty Two   21 | 22 | 16 | $8
1219 Granville St. (bet. Davie & Drake Sts.), 604-688-5494;
www.ginger62.com
The "hot crowd without all the little kiddies is a bonus" at this
"sexy" '60s-inspired Downtowner with an "intimate feel"; start
the evening with global small plates, and "don't expect to get in if
you come too late" because this "casual-but-upscale" joint is a
"favourite place to cool out."

900 West   20 | 23 | 18 | $12
Fairmont Hotel Vancouver, 900 W. Georgia St. (bet. Burrard &
Hornby Sts.), 604-684-3131; www.fairmont.com
Suits and suitors alike appreciate this "fine, functional" lounge
Downtown in the historic Fairmont that's a "pretty" spot "for a
drink or two" and "good bar snacks"; it's "appropriate for business meetings" when "you don't want too informal an atmosphere", but the setting is also "romantic" enough "to start or end
the evening with someone special."

Odyssey   17 | 12 | 14 | $8
1251 Howe St. (bet. Davie & Drake Sts.), 604-689-5256;
www.theodysseynightclub.com
"Don't miss the shower show" urge eager sorts at this Downtown
"techno" club/cabaret, where "friendly, gorgeous" "older" guys
come for drag queens, male strippers and "partying"; "the big

fish in a small pond of gay nightlife options in Vancouver", it still has a few fussy fellows finding it "pretty scuzzy."

OPUS BAR
23 | 23 | 20 | $14

Opus Hotel, 322 Davie St. (bet. Hamilton & Mainland Sts.), 604-642-6787; www.opushotel.com

"Keep your paparazzi eyes open" at this "sexy" "hangout" for "movie stars" in Yaletown; an "upscale lounge with abundant eye candy" peddling "the ultimate in cool and hipness", it's "so trendy you'll want to spit" – just don't get so caught up with the "beautiful people" that you forget to "monitor your date on the bathroom TVs."

Plaza Club, The
17 | 16 | 16 | $7

881 Granville St. (bet. Robson & Smithe Sts.), 604-646-0064; www.plazaclub.net

"Party with 1,000 of your closest friends" at this "dressier" club Downtown that attracts a mixed-age crowd for mainstream tunes; while some "really like" the "changing themes" and "megawatt, pounding dance floor", spoilsports "don't get why it's so packed."

Railway Club, The
24 | 18 | 17 | $8

579 Dunsmuir St. (Seymour St.), 604-681-1625; www.therailwayclub.com

Hop aboard for "all the best local bands" – from "up-and-coming acts" to "established alternative" groups – at Downtown's "best small venue for live music"; it's a "favourite" "hip arts-scene hangout" for "all ages" who appreciate the "unpretentious atmosphere" and a staff that "makes you feel welcome."

Richards on Richards
17 | 16 | 19 | $10

1036 Richards St. (bet. Helmcken & Nelson Sts.), 604-688-1099; www.richardsonrichards.com

They "bring in lots of good acts" to this Downtown music club that a "diverse crowd" says is "a fun place for a show"; still, despite "tons of mingling" among singles "looking for a rich man or a high-class woman", a few find this "landmark" "tarnished."

Rossini's
– | – | – | E

162 Water St. (bet. Abbott & Cambie Sts.), 604-408-1300
1525 Yew St. (bet. Cornwall & York Aves.), 604-737-8080
www.rossinis.bc.ca

"When there's a smokin' jazz combo playing", each of these spots has a "great atmosphere" for dinner and live tunes; they may be more Italian "restaurant and lounge than nightclub", but supporters swear that the West Side and Gastown locations "are both nice."

Shark Club 20 | 17 | 16 | $7
180 W. Georgia St. (bet. Beatty & Cambie Sts.), 604-687-4275
4399 Lougheed Hwy. (Rosser Ave S.), Burnaby, 604-628-5500
20169 88 Ave. (202 St.), Langley, 604-513-8600
www.sharkclubs.com
"Grab a brew" and "whoop it up" at these "laid-back" sports bars that succeed when they "stick to the basics" of "TV, cold draft and reliable meals"; later, they turn into "high-end" clubs, but for game sharks, they're about "the Canucks getting their butts kicked."

Yale Hotel, The 20 | 14 | 16 | $8
1300 Granville St. (Pacific St.), 604-681-9253; www.theyale.ca
The "rough-around-the-edges" room may "need a revamp", but it "fits the music" at this "historic blues bar" in an 1885 building Downtown that "brings in world-class acts"; "all kinds of people" insist it's "great" during weekend afternoon jams, and, perhaps because it's "not too pretty", it's "less expensive than other places."

VICTORIA & VANCOUVER ISLAND

Bengal Lounge 28 | 28 | 24 | $18
Fairmont Empress Hotel, 721 Government St. (bet. Belleville & Humboldt Sts.), Victoria, 250-389-2727; www.fairmont.com
"You'd think you were in colonial India" at this "ritzy" Downtowner, a "historic place" to sip "a Tiger's Kiss martini as you listen to live jazz" on weekends and imagine you're "rich and famous"; it's "not where you want to have to buy your own drink", but the "combination of ale on draft with the curry of the day" is "pure heaven."

Shark Club 20 | 17 | 16 | $7
2852 Douglas St. (bet. Garbally Rd. & Market St.), Victoria, 250-386-5888; www.sharkclubs.com
See review in Vancouver section.

Sticky Wicket Pub & Restaurant ∇ 22 | 21 | 21 | $9
Strathcona Hotel, 919 Douglas St. (Courtney St.), Victoria, 250-383-7137; www.strathconahotel.com
"People of all ages" go to bat for this "huge", "friendly" pub, one of seven sports-themed rooms in Victoria's "biggest conglomeration

of clubs", all in the Strathcona Hotel; it's "a great place" to "sit with friends" and "watch all the strangeness go by" Downtown.

WHISTLER

Dubh Linn Gate Irish Pub <u>23</u> <u>18</u> <u>17</u> <u>$9</u>
Pan Pacific Lodge, 170-4320 Sundial Cres. (off Blackcomb Way), 604-905-4047; www.dubhlinngate.com
Just "steps from the gondola" in Whistler's Pan Pacific Lodge, this "hangout" is "a perfect place to relish a pint of Guinness after a hard day on the slopes"; there's a "superb selection of beers", so "it's the right idea" "for a quick drink or a long evening", even if the "faux"-Irish setting is "antiseptic."

Garibaldi Lift Co. Bar & Grill <u>23</u> <u>19</u> <u>18</u> <u>$10</u>
Whistler Village, Springs Ln. (Whistler Way), 604-905-2220
"Watch skiers finish their runs, cheer on your favourite sports team" or sit "beside the fireplace" and listen to live music at this slopeside bar above the gondola base that's "one of the best après-ski locales" in Whistler; it "attracts a mature crowd", perhaps because it's "not so much a nightclub as a place to lounge."

Longhorn Saloon <u>20</u> <u>15</u> <u>15</u> <u>$11</u>
Carleton Lodge, 4284 Mountain Sq. (Horstman Ln.), 604-932-5999; www.longhornsaloon.ca
The "huge patio" "fills up" at this Carleton Lodge "favourite for après ski"; "get there early" and "head to the bar to order your own drinks" – otherwise, "service can be slow", since the staff "has a hard time getting around" the hordes.

Attractions

VANCOUVER

Most Popular

1. Stanley Park
2. Vancouver Aquarium
3. Museum of Anthro./UBC
4. Capilano Bridge
5. Dr. Sun Yat-Sen/Gdn.

Top Appeal

27 Stanley Park
26 Museum of Anthro./UBC
    Vancouver Aquarium
25 Telus World of Science
24 VanDusen Botanical

A	P	S	$
23	23	23	M

Burnaby Village Museum
6501 Deer Lake Ave. (bet. Canada Way & Deer Lake Pl.), Burnaby; 604-293-6500; www.burnabyvillagemuseum.ca
Visitors to this "gorgeous" Burnaby living-history museum take a "walk back in time" in a 1920s village, complete with a restored

carousel and a working blacksmith's forge; a "friendly staff and volunteers" add to the experience, though some quibble that this "small" site is "more of a pit stop than an ultimate destination for a kids' day out."

Capilano Suspension Bridge　　　23 | 20 | 17 | M

3735 Capilano Rd., North Vancouver; 604-985-7474; www.capbridge.com
"Not for the faint of heart", a walk across this "swaying bridge" "nuzzling the towering pines" above North Vancouver's Capilano River "quickens the pulse"; thrill-seekers on "a natural high" feel like they're "on top of the world", but unimpressed amblers argue that it costs "too much money" for "a lot of hoopla" when you can "head to Lynn Canyon's" span and get "the same feeling for free."

Dr. Sun Yat-Sen Classical　　　22 | 20 | 17 | I
Chinese Garden

578 Carrall St. (bet. Keefer Pl. & W. Pender St.); 604-662-3207; www.vancouverchinesegarden.com
"An oasis of calm" on the edge of "bustling" Chinatown, this "classical Chinese garden", with its "little winding paths", "beautiful rock" arrangements and "fascinating botanicals", is a "contemplative" spot; "bring your camera", take a tour (the guides' "knowledge, history and perspective make the trip worthwhile") and "access your Zen-like state."

Granville Island　　　　　　　　– | – | – | $0

Anderson St. (under the Granville St. Bridge); 604-666-5784; www.granvilleisland.com
Anchored by the foodie's paradise of the Public Market, this pedestrian-friendly peninsula that was once an industrial wasteland on the West Side is now a top attraction; browse the eclectic galleries, museums, theatres, restaurants and marine supply stores, or simply admire the city views from the shores of False Creek.

Grouse Mountain　　　　　　　　– | – | – | E

6400 Nancy Greene Way (Grousewoods Dr.), North Vancouver; 604-984-0661; www.grousemountain.com
Its lights seen for miles around, this North Vancouver peak with stunning panoramas and an array of activities is only a 15-minute drive from Downtown; ride the tram to ski day or night (December–April), take in a lumberjack show or go hiking before hanging out on the picturesque patio at the bistro.

Museum of Anthropology at UBC   26 | 25 | 21 | I

*University of British Columbia, 6393 NW Marine Dr. (bet. E. Mall &
W. Mall); 604-822-5087; www.moa.ubc.ca*

Amateur ethnographers seeking "a crash course" in local
"aboriginal history" "could spend days and only scratch the sur-
face" of this "scholars' treasure trove" housed in Arthur Erickson's
"stunning" West Side masterpiece; "fabulous totem poles",
"phenomenal" artifacts, the "spectacular" longhouse and world-
famous sculptor Bill Reid's 'The Raven and the First Men' make it
"a must-see."

STANLEY PARK   27 | 22 | 18 | $0

*Entrances at Beach Ave. (Lagoon Dr.) and W. George Ave. (Chilco St.);
604-257-8400; www.city.vancouver.bc.ca/parks/parks/stanley*

"Bring your walking shoes" to this "jewel in Vancouver's crown",
a "serene urban oasis" where the mountain views are "breathtaking" and the ways to enjoy yourself are "endless"; "locals"
who "love it" for "hiking, biking, swimming and sunning" (and
who voted it the *Vancouver Survey*'s Most Popular attraction)
suggest that whether you "walk the seawall" or "just hang out",
it's "the essence of what this great city is all about."

Telus World of Science   25 | 24 | 22 | M

(fka Science World)
*1455 Quebec St. (Terminal Ave.); 604-443-7443;
www.scienceworld.bc.ca*

"Your kids go wild" amidst the "wonderful" "interactive displays"
"that make learning cool" in this "spherical" East Side building
that "looks like a giant golf ball at the end of False Creek"; it's
a "great way to spend a rainy afternoon", especially if you take
in an "amazing" IMAX show – just "try to go on a quiet day" because "it can be a zoo."

VANCOUVER AQUARIUM   26 | 24 | 21 | M
MARINE SCIENCE CENTRE

*Stanley Park, 845 Avison Way (Aquarium Way); 604-659-3474;
www.vanaqua.org*

"Don't expect killer whales playing the tuba" – the "entertaining"
yet "informative" exhibits are "designed for education" at
Stanley Park's "compact", "captivating" marine facility; the "expert trainers" display "a lot of concern for the animals", and the
place is "packed with things to do", so plan to spend at least "half

a day interacting" with the "delightfully fun sea otters" and "humanlike belugas" at this "kids' favourite."

Vancouver Art Gallery   23 | 22 | 19 | M |
750 Hornby St. (bet. Robson & W. Georgia Sts.); 604-662-4719;
www.vanartgallery.bc.ca
From the "first-rate temporary exhibits" to a permanent collection that's strong on "fabulous" works by BC artist Emily Carr, "the curators do a wonderful job" at this "lovely" Downtown museum; though size queens "wish it were bigger", admirers assert that it's "attractive for locals and world travelers alike", particularly if you refuel in the "great cafe" or go on a pay-what-you-wish Tuesday evening.

Vancouver Maritime Museum   22 | 20 | 19 | I |
1905 Ogden Ave. (Chestnut St.); 604-737-2621;
www.vancouvermaritimemuseum.com
A "must-see for kids" (or anyone) "with an interest in ships", this small but "surprisingly" good West Side waterfront museum is "a unique attraction with interesting, novel" marine exhibits; a highlight is a climb aboard the historic schooner St. Roch, the first vessel to navigate the Northwest Passage both ways.

Vancouver Museum   ▽ 20 | 20 | 20 | I |
Vanier Park, 1100 Chestnut St. (Whyte St.); 604-736-4431;
www.vanmuseum.bc.ca
In the West Side's Vanier Park, this "interesting" museum with a cone-shaped roof that resembles a Coast Salish hat explores "everything on the origins of the West Coast"; a staff that's "passionate about Canadian history" channels enthusiasm into the "unique displays", so if critics crab that it's "not world-class", it's still "one of Vancouver's little-known gems."

VanDusen Botanical Garden   24 | 21 | 20 | M |
5251 Oak St. (W. 37th Ave.); 604-878-9274;
www.vandusengarden.org
"You can count on beauty each time you visit" the "peaceful", "well-kept grounds" of this "fantastic" West Side "treasure" filled with "rare, delicate" plants; "bring a picnic" or enjoy a "romantic" meal in the "quaint" Shaughnessy Restaurant, but don't miss the "awesome spring flower expositions", the "great" Elizabethan maze or December's "wonderful" Festival of Lights.

VICTORIA & VANCOUVER ISLAND

BUTCHART GARDENS, THE   28 | 26 | 22 | M |
800 Benvenuto Ave. (Wallace Dr.), Brentwood Bay; 866-652-4422;
www.butchartgardens.com
"A virtual fairyland of flowers", this "don't-miss" ranks among "the most magnificent" of its kind, with "beautiful botanical displays" that include a "breathtaking Sunken Garden"; Saanich's patch of "pure heaven" is a "lovely place to walk", and since "children have endless" expanses "to explore", it's "not just for old codgers"; an "elaborate" afternoon tea is served in the Dining Room, and in summer it's "worth a second trip" for the Saturday night fireworks.

Butterfly Gardens   22 | 20 | 19 | M |
461 Benvenuto Ave. (Garden Gate Dr.), Brentwood Bay;
250-652-3822; 877-722-0272; www.butterflygardens.com
"Remember your camera" when you visit this "small but charming" tropical Sannich showcase, where "exotic" butterflies "land on your hand"; "dress lightly" since "it can get hot and humid in the observatory", and "bring your kiddies" – unless flying insects "creep them out."

Craigdarroch Castle   23 | 22 | 21 | M |
1050 Joan Cres. (bet. Fort St. & Rockland Ave.), Victoria;
250-592-5323; www.craigdarrochcastle.com
Luckily for her, the wife of Robert Dunsmuir (the BC coal baron who built this "imposing" mansion) "wasn't expected to vacuum", though she probably enjoyed the "gorgeous views from the top floor", and she might've liked the "excellent" self-guided tours nowadays; this "fascinating" 1890s building a 30-minute walk from Downtown is full of "good stories", but it's especially "beautiful" when decorated "during the holidays."

Royal British Columbia Museum   27 | 27 | 22 | M |
675 Belleville St. (bet. Douglas & Government Sts.), Victoria;
888-447-7977; www.royalbcmuseum.bc.ca
Visitors "of all ages" "soak up all that is West Coast Canada" in the "spectacular exhibits" at this "wonderful" Downtown museum, a "winner" for "sensory delight"; the "outstanding First Nations items" and "dioramas alone are worth the price of admission", and the natural history section (with its "infamous wooly mammoth") is "excellent", so "take all day" to explore this "national treasure."

Hotels

VANCOUVER

R	S	D	P	$
23	24	22	23	$294

**Fairmont Hotel
Vancouver, The** ✗Ⓗ🐾ⓢ⚳≋
900 W. Georgia St.; 604-684-3131; fax 662-1929; 800-441-1414; www.fairmont.com; 536 rooms, 20 suites
Emanating "elegance" from the "grand lobby" to the "English-style rooms", this 1939 Downtown "landmark" is "perfectly situated to get the most out of the city", particularly if you're on "a shopaholics

holiday"; the staff "spoils you", and "like an old lady trying to keep up", this "dowager" works hard for her "charms."

Fairmont 24 | 24 | 20 | 23 | $369
Waterfront, The ⊕✻🏌🏊
900 Canada Place Way; 604-691-1991; fax 691-1999; 800-441-1414; www.fairmont.com; 459 rooms, 30 suites
An "obvious choice if you're going on a cruise" but "well-located for touring the city as well", this "modern" "waterfront" tower is all about the "stunning" "five-star" vistas; many of the "expansive" rooms boast "floor-to-ceiling windows", and the "helpful" staff keeps things shipshape, though a few knock the "institutional" building that gets "crowded with throngs of ship passengers."

Four Seasons ✕🏌🏊 25 | 27 | 25 | 24 | $335
791 W. Georgia St.; 604-689-9333; fax 684-4555; 800-332-3442; www.fourseasons.com; 294 rooms, 66 suites
The "flawless" service wins raves from reviewers who always feel "pampered" at this "first-class hotel"; the "convenient Downtown location" is handy "for business travelers", who find the power dining "wonderfully delicious" and unwind in the indoor-outdoor rooftop pool; the "'70s throwback" building is "not much to look at", but inside, it has all the "Four Seasons touches."

Opus Hotel ✕✻🏌 26 | 24 | 25 | 22 | $330
322 Davie St.; 604-642-6787; fax 642-6780; 866-642-6787; www.opushotel.com; 84 rooms, 12 suites
"Put the blinds down" in the "street-facing bathrooms" at this "one-of-a-kind" boutique hotel in "trendy" Yaletown – "the place in Vancouver to see and be seen"; from the "refreshingly" "hip" rooms, done in "funky", vibrant hues, to the "hot" lobby bar where you're apt to "run into movie stars" to the classic French brasserie, Elixir, the scene is "sexy and modern."

Pacific Palisades ⌂✻🏌Ⓢ🏊 23 | 20 | 18 | 21 | $223
1277 Robson St.; 604-688-0461; fax 688-4374; 800-663-1815; www.pacificpalisadeshotel.com; 233 suites
Fans of the Miami "retro look" go gaga for the "quirky decor" and "bold colors" at this "fun" Downtowner, where the "spacious suites" are "very comfortable, especially for longer stays", and you'll have "terrific views of the Vancouver skyline" if your room

is high enough; run by a "helpful staff", it's a "true value" on "the best shopping street in town."

Pan Pacific 🏊⑤♨   25 23 22 25 $376
300-999 Canada Pl.; 604-662-8111; fax 685-8690; 800-937-1515; www.panpac.com; 465 rooms, 39 suites
"If you stay in one of the suites" with "stunning views", "you'll never want to leave" this "nautical-styled" "paradise" in a "fabulous waterfront location" "atop the cruise-ship terminal"; you can "swim outside overlooking the harbour and the mountains" and ignore the "huge bustling lobby full of conventioneers and cruisers", but landlubbers wish it were a bit "closer to the city action."

Sutton Place Hotel 🏨🏊⑤♨   23 24 22 23 $342
845 Burrard St.; 604-682-5511; fax 682-5513; 866-378-8866; www.suttonplace.com; 350 rooms, 47 suites
"Grab a drink and stargaze" in the lounge at this "Hollywood North hotel" that's "popular with movie and TV types"; business travelers overlook the "old-fashioned" rooms, and give the "excellent service" and Downtown location a "thumbs-up", while sweet tooths savour the "sinful" Thursday–Saturday chocolate bar.

Wedgewood ⑤   –   –   –   – $307
845 Hornby St.; 604-689-7777; fax 608-5348; 800-663-0666; www.wedgewoodhotel.com; 41 rooms, 42 suites
Edwardian luxury is alive and well in Downtown Vancouver at this chic boutique; all dark woods and crystal chandeliers, the lobby and lounge (popular for power cocktails) recall the Queen's parlors, while the guestrooms are plush, if a bit subdued; the Bacchus restaurant features French creations, and there's an on-site spa.

Westin Bayshore 🏨🏊♨   23 22 18 23 $338
1601 Bayshore Dr.; 604-682-3377; fax 687-3102; 800-937-8461; www.westin.com; 510 rooms
"Jog out the back door" to the seawall for an "exceptional" workout, when you stay at this sprawling property on Coal Harbour, "a stone's throw from Stanley Park"; it has "beautiful views of the marina and the mountains", "well-appointed rooms" and business-friendly service, as well as "great conference facilities"; just beware that there are "virtually negligible dining options."

Westin Grand ♔♙♨♨♒♒　　24 | 22 | 19 | 22 | $306
433 Robson St.; 604-602-1999; fax 647-2502; 800-937-8461;
www.westin.com; 207 suites
You might not realize that this "chic" "all-suite hotel" is "shaped
like a grand piano", but you will notice it's got a "clever design",
including "practical" mini-kitchens tucked into the walls; athletic
types "love the fitness facilities and outdoor pool", and the
Downtown location is "excellent for business."

VICTORIA & VANCOUVER ISLAND

Aerie Resort ✕♙♒♒♒♒　　25 | 25 | 26 | 22 | $295
600 Ebedora Ln., Malahat; 250-743-7115; fax 743-4766;
800-518-1933; www.aerie.bc.ca; 9 rooms, 27 suites
"Divine location, views and dining" sums up this "beautiful"
Relais & Châteaux "haven" 30 minutes from Victoria; proponents
praise the "impeccable service" and "lovely rooms with balconies
overlooking the forest", advising "get a suite with a sunken tub."

Hastings House ✕♙♒♒　　27 | 27 | 27 | 24 | $420
160 Upper Ganges Rd., Salt Spring Island; 250-537-2362; fax 537-5333;
800-661-9255; www.hastingshouse.com; 16 suites, 2 cottages
From the "hot muffins at your doorstep" to fires at night, "this is
the place to be pampered", a "romantic" Relais & Châteaux property on "charming" Salt Spring Island that garnered an
International Hotels Survey's No. 1 ranking in Canada; modernists
prefer "the newer hillside suites", though the 1938 manor house is
"cosy" too; add a "first-class kitchen" that turns out some of "the
best dinners west of the Rockies", and the entirety is "sublime."

Sooke Harbour House ♒♒　　– | – | – | – | $312
1528 Whiffen Spit Rd., Sooke; 250-642-3421; fax 642-6988;
www.sookeharbourhouse.com; 28 rooms, 3 suites
Surrounded by the Pacific and colourful gardens, this homey
Sooke inn, 45 minutes from Victoria, features unique quarters
with antiques, rock fireplaces and soaking tubs with sea views;
every guestroom comes with a bottle of port and several pairs of
rainboots to encourage exploration of the extensive grounds, and
outdoorsy types can fish, see salmon spawn, tour wineries, hike
and whale watch.

Wickaninnish Inn ✕👥⌐Ⓢ   26 | 26 | 26 | 26 |$440

Osprey Ln., Tofino; 250-725-3100; fax 725-3110; 800-333-4604;
www.wickinn.com; 75 rooms
"Bring someone to snuggle with" at this "secluded" Relais &
Châteaux "getaway" that's "integrated" into Vancouver Island's
"rugged" western coast; the "stunning rooms" have "killer Pacific
vistas", and the staff "pays attention to details" – from "binocu-
lars to watch the ships" to bath salts, candles, even raincoats; to
top it off, the Pointe Restaurant offers "sensational" Northwest
fare, so "mortgage your house, sell your first born" – it's "worth it."

WHISTLER

Fairmont Chateau   24 | 25 | 22 | 27 |$445
Whistler, The 👥🏌👥⌐Ⓢ⛷🏊🎾

4599 Chateau Blvd.; 604-938-8000; fax 938-2291; 800-441-1414;
www.fairmont.com; 490 rooms, 60 suites
"The most elegant way to experience Whistler" may be this "perfect blend of refinement and ruggedness", a "cosy" "lodge with
big-city touches"; come winter, it's "ski-in/ski-out luxury" "right
at the foot of the mountain", and in milder times, it's "paradise"
"for sightseeing and golf" at a Robert Trent Jones, Jr. course.

Four Seasons Whistler 👥Ⓢ⛷🏊   – | – | – | – |$845

4591 Blackcomb Way; 604-935-3400; fax 935-3455;
www.fourseasons.com; 175 rooms, 95 suites, 3 townhouses
Photo-ready scenery is one reason vacationers trek to this alpine
retreat in Whistler; once here, guests are treated to warm, wood
interiors with in-room fireplaces, endless spa treatments and skiing nearby on some of the world's best slopes.

Pan Pacific Whistler   – | – | – | – |$698
Village Centre 🍽👥Ⓢ⛷🏊

4229 Blackcomb Way; 604-966-5500; fax 966-5501;
www.panpacific.com; 83 suites
In the middle of posh Whistler is this Pan Pacific boutique, a modern
affair with rooms that feature full kitchens, gas fireplaces and
soaking tubs; fuel up at the breakfast buffet before hitting the
slopes, then load up on afternoon hors d'oeuvres before enjoying
the heated pool, outdoor hot tubs or Vital Spirit spa.

Indexes

CUISINES
RESTAURANT LOCATIONS
NIGHTLIFE LOCATIONS
HOTEL LOCATIONS

Places outside of Vancouver are marked as follows:
(V&V=Victoria & Vancouver Island; W=Whistler).

CUISINES

Asian Fusion
Ch'i
Stella's

Barbecue
Memphis Blues BBQ
Tomahawk BBQ

Belgian
Chambar

Chinese
(* dim sum specialist)
Imperial Chinese*
J & J Wonton/V&V
Kirin Mandarin*
Kirin Seafood*
Pink Pearl Chinese*
Shanghai Chinese*
Shao-Lin Noodle
Sun Sui Wah*
Szechuan Chongqing
Wild Rice

Coffee Shops/Diners
Diner
Tomahawk BBQ

Continental
Edgewater Lodge/W
Pear Tree
William Tell

Dessert
Fleuri
Griffins
Trafalgar's Bistro

Eclectic
Bin 941/942
Blue Fox Cafe/V&V
Diner
glowbal grill
Habit Lounge
Nu
Rebar Modern/V&V
Sobo/V&V
Stella's
Trafalgar's Bistro

European (Modern)
Après/W
Parkside

French
Aerie Resort/V&V
Bacchus
Cassis Bistro
Deep Cove Chalet/V&V
Five Sails
Fleuri
Hermitage
La Belle Auberge
Le Crocodile
Lumière
Paprika Bistro/V&V
Provence Marina
Provence Med.
Restaurant Matisse/V&V
Salade de Fruits
Saveur

French (Bistro)
Bacchus Bistro
Bistro Pastis
Brasserie L'Ecole/V&V

Café de Paris
La Regalade
Mistral Bistro

French (New)
Val d'Isère/W

Greek
Kalamata Greek Taverna
Stepho's Souvlaki
Takis Taverna

Hamburgers
Splitz Grill/W
Vera's Burger

Hungarian
Paprika Bistro/V&V

Indian
Maurya Indian
Vij's
Vij's Rangoli

Italian
(N=Northern)
Adesso Bistro
Amarcord
Cafe Il Nido
Caffe de Medici
Circolo
Don Francesco
Il Caminetto/Umberto/W (N)
Il Giardino/Umberto (N)
Il Terrazzo/V&V (N)
La Terrazza
Lombardo's
Marcello
Pagliacci's/V&V

Quattro at Whistler/W
Quattro on Fourth
Tratt. di Umberto/W
Villa del Lupo
Water St. Café
Zambri's/V&V

Japanese
(* sushi specialist)
EN Japanese
Gyoza King
Hapa Izakaya
Kitanoya Guu
Kobe Japanese
Shijo Japanese*
Shiro Japanese*
Shiru-Bay
Sushi Village/W*
Sushi Ya/W*
ToJo's*
Toshi*

Lebanese
Habibi's

Malaysian
Tropika Malaysian

Mediterranean
Caramba!/W
CinCin
Cioppino's
Provence Med.
Savory Coast

Mexican
Lolita's Cantina
Topanga Cafe

Nuevo Latino
Century

Pacific Northwest
Aerie Resort/V&V
Aqua Riva
Araxi/W
Arbutus Grille/V&V
Aubergine Grille/W
Aurora Bistro
Beach Hse./Pier
Beach Side Cafe
Bear Foot Bistro/W
Bishop's
Brix
Cafe Brio/V&V
Camille's/V&V
Chartwell
Ch'i
Cru
Delilah's
Diva at the Met
Dock 503/V&V
Edgewater Lodge/W
Empress Room/V&V
Feenie's
Fiddlehead Joe's
Fifty Two 80 Bistro/W
Five Sails
Globe @ YVR
Griffins
Hart House
Hastings House/V&V
Herons
Horizons/Burnaby
La Rua/W
Lift
Marina/V&V
Ocean 6 Seventeen

O'Doul's
Pescatore Seafood/V&V
Pointe/Wickaninnish/V&V
Raincity Grill
Rare
Rim Rock Cafe/W
Rosemeade/V&V
Salmon House
Seasons Hill Top
Sequoia Grill
Sooke Harbour/V&V
Tapastree
Temple/V&V
Tomato Fresh Food
Villa del Lupo
Watermark/Kits
Water St. Café
West
Wildflower/W
Wild Garlic

Pizza
Lombardo's
Marcello
Nat's NY Pizzeria

Portuguese
Senova

Pub Food
Cardero's

Seafood
Blue Crab B&G/V&V
Blue Water Cafe
Cannery
Coast
C Restaurant
Ferris' Oyster Bar/V&V
Fish Hse./Stanley Park

Go Fish!
Imperial Chinese
Joe Fortes
Kirin Seafood
Marina/V&V
Monk's Grill/W
Pajo's
Pescatore Seafood/V&V
Rim Rock Cafe/W
Rodney's Oyster
Sun Sui Wah

Singaporean
Tropika Malaysian

Spanish
(* tapas specialist)
Senova*

Steakhouses
Gotham Steak
Hy's Encore

Hy's Steak/W
Joe Fortes
Keg Steakhouse/V&V/W
Kobe Japanese
Monk's Grill/W
Morton's Steak
Saltlik Steak

Swiss
William Tell

Thai
Montri's Thai
Salathai Thai
Sawasdee Thai
Siam Thai/V&V
Simply Thai
Tropika Malaysian

Vegetarian
Habibi's
Rebar Modern/V&V

RESTAURANT LOCATIONS

VANCOUVER

Burnaby
Hart House
Horizons/Burnaby
Keg Steakhouse
Pear Tree

Coquitlam
Kirin Seafood

Delta
Keg Steakhouse

Downtown
Aqua Riva
Bacchus
Cafe Il Nido
Caffe de Medici
Cassis Bistro
Century
Chambar
Chartwell
CinCin
C Restaurant

Diva at the Met
Don Francesco
Fiddlehead Joe's
Five Sails
Fleuri
Gotham Steak
Griffins
Hermitage
Herons
Hy's Encore
Il Giardino/Umberto
Imperial Chinese
Joe Fortes
Keg Steakhouse
Kirin Mandarin
Kitanoya Guu
Kobe Japanese
Le Crocodile
Morton's Steak
Nu
O'Doul's
Rare
Salathai Thai
Saltlik Steak
Saveur
Shanghai Chinese
Tropika Malaysian
Villa del Lupo
Wild Rice
William Tell

East Side
Aurora Bistro
Cannery
Ch'i
Habit Lounge
Lombardo's
Marcello
Memphis Blues BBQ

Pink Pearl Chinese
Sawasdee Thai
Stella's
Sun Sui Wah
Szechuan Chongqing
Toshi

Gastown
Water St. Café

Granville Island
Keg Steakhouse

Ladner
La Belle Auberge

Langley
Bacchus Bistro

New Westminster
Keg Steakhouse

North Vancouver
Tomahawk BBQ

Port Moody
Pajo's

Richmond
Globe @ YVR
Keg Steakhouse
Kirin Seafood
Sun Sui Wah
Tropika Malaysian

Steveston
Pajo's

Surrey
Keg Steakhouse

Tsawwassen
Pajo's

West End
Bin 941 Tapas
Café de Paris
Cardero's
Delilah's
Fish Hse./Stanley Park
Gyoza King
Habibi's
Hapa Izakaya
Lift
Lolita's Cantina
Nat's NY Pizzeria
Parkside
Raincity Grill
Savory Coast
Sequoia Grill
Stepho's Souvlaki
Takis Taverna
Tapastree
Vera's Burger
Wild Garlic

West Side
Adesso Bistro
Bin 942 Tapas
Bishop's
Bistro Pastis
Cru
EN Japanese
Feenie's
Go Fish!
Kalamata Greek Taverna
Kirin Seafood
Lumière
Maurya Indian
Memphis Blues BBQ

Mistral Bistro
Montri's Thai
Nat's NY Pizzeria
Ocean 6 Seventeen
Provence Med.
Quattro on Fourth
Salade de Fruits
Salathai Thai
Seasons Hill Top
Senova
Shao-Lin Noodle
Shijo Japanese
Shiro Japanese
ToJo's
Tomato Fresh Food
Topanga Cafe
Trafalgar's Bistro
Tropika Malaysian
Vera's Burger
Vij's
Vij's Rangoli
Watermark/Kits
West
Wild Garlic

West Vancouver
Beach Hse./Pier
Beach Side Cafe
Keg Steakhouse
La Regalade
Salmon House
Vera's Burger

Yaletown
Amarcord
Blue Water Cafe
Brix
Cioppino's
Circolo

Coast
Diner
glowbal grill
La Terrazza

Provence Marina
Rodney's Oyster
Shiru-Bay
Simply Thai

VICTORIA & VANCOUVER ISLAND

Brentwood Bay
Arbutus Grille

Malahat
Aerie Resort

Downtown
Blue Crab B&G
Blue Fox Cafe
Brasserie L'Ecole
Cafe Brio
Camille's
Empress Room
Ferris' Oyster Bar
Il Terrazzo
J & J Wonton
Keg Steakhouse
Pagliacci's
Pescatore Seafood
Rebar Modern
Restaurant Matisse
Siam Thai
Temple
Zambri's

Oak Bay
Marina
Paprika Bistro

Saanich
Keg Steakhouse

Salt Spring Island
Hastings House

Sidney
Deep Cove Chalet
Dock 503

Sooke
Sooke Harbour

Tofino
Pointe/Wickaninnish
Sobo

Esquimalt
Rosemeade

WHISTLER

Après
Araxi
Aubergine Grille
Bear Foot Bistro
Caramba!

Edgewater Lodge
Fifty Two 80 Bistro
Hy's Steak
Il Caminetto/Umberto
Keg Steakhouse

La Rua
Monk's Grill
Quattro at Whistler
Rim Rock Cafe
Splitz Grill

Sushi Village
Sushi Ya
Tratt. di Umberto
Val d'Isère
Wildflower

NIGHTLIFE LOCATIONS

VANCOUVER

Burnaby
Shark Club

Downtown
AuBar Nightclub
Bacchus Lounge
Cellar Nightclub
Commodore Ballrm.
Crush Champagne
Ginger Sixty Two
900 West
Odyssey
Plaza Club
Railway Club
Richards on Richards
Shark Club

Yale Hotel

Gastown
Rossini's

Langley
Shark Club

West End
Celebrities

West Side
Rossini's

Yaletown
Bar None
Opus Bar

VICTORIA & VANCOUVER ISLAND

Downtown
Bengal Lounge

Shark Club
Sticky Wicket Pub

WHISTLER

Dubh Linn Gate
Garibaldi Lift B&G

Longhorn Saloon

HOTEL LOCATIONS

VANCOUVER

Downtown
Fairmont
Fairmont Waterfront
Four Seasons
Pacific Palisades
Pan Pacific
Sutton Place

Wedgewood
Westin Bayshore
Westin Grand

Yaletown
Opus

VICTORIA & VANCOUVER ISLAND

Malahat
Aerie

Salt Spring Island
Hastings House

Sooke
Sooke Harbour

Tofino
Wickaninnish Inn

WHISTLER

Fairmont Chateau
Four Seasons Whistler

Pan Pacific Whistler